# HOW THEY OWNED A BOAT AND DIDN'T SPEND ANY MONEY

AUTHOR/ILLUSTRATOR
Carlo DiNapoli

HAWK PUBLISHING AND DISTRIBUTING
Birmingham, AL
Longboat Key, FL

**OTHER WORKS BY CARLO DINAPOLI:**
The Cajun Gourmet Afloat and On the Road, 8th printing
Cooking Country with Shotgun Red, 1st printing
All I Ever Wanted to Know About Cooking I Learned From Momma, 4th printing
The Upper Crud Cookbook, 4th printing
Is This Country Cooking? This is Country Cooking!, 2nd printing

**COMING SOON:**
The Damned Well Do's and Don'ts for a Perfect Lifestyle
Yankee Cooking Conch and Dem Other Critters

**OTHER WORKS BY PEN NAME, JONATHAN WOE:**
The Wing'ed Whale from Woefully
The Longneck Bird of Longboat Key, One of the Privileged Class

Copyright © 1990
Revised
April 1993, Second Printing

HAWK PUBLISHING & DISTR.
P.O. Box 8422
Longboat Key, FL 34228

Printed in the United States of America

All rights reserved. No part of this book may be reproduced or transmitted in any form or by any means, electronic or mechanical, including photocopying, recording or any information storage and retrieval system, without permission in writing from the publisher.

All the characters, places and events in this book are fictitious and any resemblance to actual persons, living or dead, or places is purely coincidental.

# DEDICATION

To my darling wife,

As long as I have her eyes to look at me, I will never need the sun to be warm.

And special thanks to the U.S. Coast Guard and the Power Squadron in their efforts to protect us pleasure boaters in our trials and tribulations upon the waterway.

# INTRODUCTION

Let me introduce these two splendid people who are the main characters in this work. I say people because they are alive to me and to all of us that go down to the sea in our boats. Bilge and Betty Scuppers were created from the many sea stories told to me when I started writing this book, as a satire on owning a boat. Each of us has had his moments of joy and misfortune on the waterway. I took an author's liberty of allowing the events in this work to happen to these two wonderful people. With these liberties, I granted them the boater's dream of never having to spend any money.

Having the experience of a licensed captain of towboats, ocean-going tugs and yachts, I felt compelled to write this work to share the joy and excitement of boating with both the full-time boater, occasional boater and would-be boater. There are portions of this book that are instructive, though humor was the only way I felt that these instructions could be presented, both valuable and lasting. The drawings are replicas of true boating rules and regulations. They are placed here to help the inexperienced boater enjoy the hilarious classes on boating.

Those who participated in the editing of this work were non-boaters. Consequently, their response of laughter, tears and astonishment convinced me this work accomplished what I set out to do. First, to entertain, second, to inform and third, to entertain.

Anyone who reads this work, boater or non-boater will meet many of those characters they already know. I changed the names of the persons in these incidents to match their virtues, characteristics and personalities. To make a point, I'm sure you have met the Commander Pompous-Ass type around the marina. What about Mr. Know-It-All, BigBoat-Bigshot and the marina manager, Mr. Daily Suffer; there is Old Ragg-Bagger, Commander May Day and many more.

You will laugh and cry, at the same time, cheer and boo and raise hell right along with our two heroes against some of the characters on the waterway and the rules and regulations of boating.

# CHAPTER ONE

Bilge and Betty Scuppers just completed thirty years of faithful service for a well known New York department store. Betty is a beauty, to hear Bilge tell it. She is five foot two, eyes of blue, 98 pounds, and as flat-chested as a ten-year-old boy. She has a cute face, a perky little behind, and so easy to fall in love with. She has one minor fault, she can never remember names.

Bilge, to hear Betty tell it, is soooooo handsome. He is six foot one, pot-bellied and stoop shouldered. He has sad, somber eyes, a long skinny nose, and is as bald as an Italian monk. He's also blessed by being pear shaped, one of his blessings...if his jacket fits over his middle, it gives him lots of room in the shoulders.

[ACTUALLY, HE LOOKS LIKE A KIND, SAD-EYED BUZZARD.]

Anyway, Bilge started his career at the store in ladies' underwear and that's where he wound up. One of his favorite sayings was, "I've seen many changes over the years." There were highs during Bilge's career. For instance, as the head man in ladies' underwear, he was given his own dong dong. That was his signal at the store to call the office so Mr. Chick-In-Sheet, his boss, wouldn't have to leave his office to chew Bilge's butt out. Also, his dong gave Bilge a pontifical feeling every time it went dong . . . dong . . . dong on the store's PA system.

Betty, on the other hand, traveled to many different departments over the life of her career. This was because she never quite understood the overwhelming technology required to complete a sales slip. This prompted Mr. Chick-In-Sheet to recommend Betty as the ideal person to head the Complaint Department. After six months on the job complaints dropped drastically and Betty became a permanent fixture in that department.

"Why bother to complain," complained the customers, "she wouldn't understand your complaint anyway."

Bilge and Betty were the ideal couple. They were alike in

temperament, and compatible as two peas in a pod. Speaking of peas, Betty would always remind people that Scuppers is spelled with 1 r and definitely 2 pees. As...Scuppeers. Pronounced...Scup-peers, by the Scuppers.

The large department store where Bilge and Betty had served faithfully through thirty years of boredom to express its generosity gave a farewell retirement party, which few of their fellow employees bothered to attend. They were given a party together, of course, to save money for the store.

While lying awake after their exciting evening at the party, they discussed many scenarios for their future. Bilge thought of becoming an active member of the Veterans of Foreign Wars. Betty thought it would be exciting to join a quilting club if she could ever learn to sew. And for memory's sake, Bilge had a dong-dong tone installed on their phone.

Ah, but Lady Luck was hovering over the happy couple. The next day they were informed that they had won a year's supply of fuel on a raffle ticket, that Mr. Chick-In-Sheet had forced Bilge to buy. Mr. Chick-In-Sheet now hated Bilge's guts more than ever, because Bilge won the prize and didn't even own a car. Mr. Chick-In-Sheet had worked diligently with the oil company to fix that raffle so his wife would win and was now determined to find whoever had dared change it to an honest raffle.

The reason Bilge didn't have a driver's license was because he had turned it in, in protest, when Betty failed her driving test three times because she refused to wear her glasses.

That night while they were in bed, Bilge's dong went off, which came as a total surprise to Betty.

"Bilge," she whispered, "who could be calling at this time of the night?"

As Bilge reached for the phone, Betty pleaded, "Bilge, please let me answer it. I just loooooove talking to people who dial the wrong number. I meet such interesting people that way." She picked up the receiver, and in her squeaky sing-song voice she answered, "Yeeessss, you have reached the Scup-peers. How may I help yoooouuuuu?"

There was a slight pause...the caller was making sure this

was really happening to him. "Mrs. Scuppers, this is Lawer Potters-A-Field down here in Florida. I hope ya'll don't mind me calling ya'll at this time of the night, ma'am."

"Oh no, Mr. Lawer Pootyfelt. I love phone calls anytime, even if they don't make any sense."

"The name is Lawer Potters-A-Field, ma'am."

"I understand now, Mr. Pottyfelt."

"No, ma'am, it's Lawer Potters-A-Field, ma'am."

Betty said politely, "You must be very proud of being a lawyer, Mr. Pottyfault, since you told me three times already."

"No, ma'am, my name is Lawer Potters-A-Field."

Betty rolled her eyes in the air in growing frustration.

"Ya'll see, my name is Lawer . . . my first name is Lawer. Everybody calls me Lawer. But I'm not a lawyer. My brother-in-law, Underwood, is the lawyer, but I own Underwood's Undertaker Parlor. I'm an undertaker, ma'am. Well, anyway, ma'am, we all been tryin' to locate ya'll. You see, my brother-in-law had ya'lls Uncle Side Scuppers. Now I have him. What we all want to know is, should I bury him?"

Always known for getting right to the point with her intelligent questions, Betty asked, "Wellllll, is he dead?"

"That fellow is plenty dead, ma'am. He's been dead three, maybe four days 'bout. He has a real nice $595.00 funeral all paid for."

"In that case, Mr. Pottypie, do it."

"Do what, ma'am?"

"Bury him of course."

"I'll do 'em under and ya'll can be proud. By the way my brother-in-law said for ya'll to call him. Ya'lls uncle dun up and left ya'll a kinda big boat."

Bilge was listening in at this time and asked, "Mr. What's Your Face, how big is a kinda big boat?"

"Bigger than most ya'll see runnin' around, but not bigger than some I've seen."

. . . . . . . . . . The pause was Bilge trying to jump-start his brain. "Oh, yes, I understand. Thank you very much for clearing that up."

After giving Bilge and Betty the lawyer's number, Lawer, who was not a lawyer, said "Bye, bye, ya'lls, have a good

5

night's sleep now."

Bilge uttered, "Betty, I couldn't sleep now if you hit me in the head with a 20-pound hammer." After hanging up the phone, he exclaimed, "Betty, did you hear what that guy said? We own a boat! We're rich!"

Betty thought for a moment and said apprehensively, "Bilge, there's a lot of talk around about how much money it takes to keep up a boat."

"Aaaah, Betty, that's a lot of bunk put out by the rich and those acting like it to keep poor people from making their playgrounds crowded. Say now, sweetie, as smart as I am, I could probably write a book on HOW TO OWN A BOAT AND NOT SPEND ANY MONEY."

"Bilge, I'm worried. Have you ever been on a boat?"

"Sure, darlin' baby girl, when I went overseas in the Army. They even let me come up out of the hole to see the ocean twice."

"Oh, that's great, baby boy. For a minute, I thought you weren't an experienced boater."

"Don't worry, Betty. Remember that guy at the store who owned a sailboat? He said there were nothing but idiots running around out there on the weekends. We shouldn't have any trouble fitting in at all. Did I say that right?"

---

The next morning, Betty and Bilge were both trying to fit an ear on one phone. Betty said, "Good morning. Is this the lawyer that's Underwood?"

"'T' which one do ya'll want, lady? Lawer or Underwood?"

"I want the lawyer who is Underwood."

"That's me, lady. What can I do for ya'll?"

"Sir, I'm Mrs. Betty Scup-peers and husband, spelled with two pees. We understand my uncle has left us a boat."

"Yes, he did . . . right down here, he did . . . clean and clear, he did . . . right down here in Florida, ma'am."

"Where in Florida, sir?"

"In Fort Lauderdale, ma'am."

"Is that near Dizzy Land?"

"Not quite, ma'am, a little further south, give or take a few hundred miles. I want ya'll to get yourselves a map, look it up for sure and come on down. Just follow the crowd, cause everybody is either comin' here or going to California."

"Betty agreed, "Oh, that's very understandable, since you both have Dizzy Lands. What more could a person want?"

"You sure are right about that, ma'am. That's all some people need, is to be in a dizzy land. We have two in Florida ma'am, one near O'lando, and the other dizzy one is called the State Capitol. Ma'am and mister, when ya'll git here go to The Sink And Sunk Boatyard. You can't miss it. They have a big sign advertising themselves right down at the water with a slogan saying, 'IN THE END YOU'll GET IT DOING BUSINESS WITH US.' Lawyer Underwood thought that the slogan needed some work until he got his bill in the end.

"All the papers are at the boatyard. Just sign them and she's yours."

Wide-eyed with delight, Betty asked, "Who is 'She'?"

"The boat. Ma'am."

"Ohhhhhhh, Bilge, how romantic. . . the boat is named 'She'?"

"Oh, no, ma'am, 'she', it's not named 'She'."

"Then what is 'She', its name?"

"MY MISTAKE, ma'am."

"What mistake?"

"'She', it is MY MISTAKE. Now ya'll got me saying it."

"Saying what, sir?"

"'She' it."

Betty instructed, "Sir, all I am trying to do is find out the name of the boat, and I don't appreciate any foul language."

"Lady, I'm not using any foul language, but if I don't use some now, I sure as hell must have given it up."

"This is Bilge speaking. Can I help you with the confusion?" Bilge was always a take-over kind of guy when it was too late.

The lawyer thought, God, what an appropriate name for this guy! He said, "Sir, I've been tryin' to tell your wife the boat's name. It's MY MISTAKE, sir."

"Weellll, Mr. Underwood, that shouldn't be any problem. If you made a mistake about the boat's name, we'll forgive you and have it corrected when we get down there."

"Yes sir, ya'll can do just that." Underwood was thinking, it sure would be nice to turn these two winners loose on those pain-in-the-behinds in the local vehicle registration office. My momma wanted me to be something honest like a politician! Maybe it's not too late to change.

Bilge asked, "Now that we have that all settled, Mr. Underwood, what is the boat's name?"

Underwood thought, there oughta be some kind of a law against this crap. "Sir, the boat's name," . . . I better be careful how I say this. I'm a good lawyer and, in spite of all I'm accused of, I should be able to tell someone something simple like a boat's name . . . "Sir, I'm gonna try to tell ya'll the boat's name. She, it . . . wait a minute, Mr. Scuppers . . . MY MISTAKE . . ." He thought, help me, God.

"Ohhhh, now I understand, Underwood, all this time you've been trying to say sheeeit, my mistake. Don't apologize, Underwood. We can get the name . . ."

Click . . . Buzzzzzzzzzzzzzzzzzzzzz

"Hello? Hello? Hello? Betty, we must have been cut off."

# CHAPTER TWO

After a frantic week of packing, they gave a tearful goodbye to their fully furnished apartment which they had rented for the last twenty-seven years. Bilge packed what clothes he thought would be necessary, and Betty packed everything. I mean everything.

They were finally off on a lovely bus trip from New York to Fort Lauderdale. The Scuppers studied the Boat U.S. catalog all the way down. By the way, they were the first people to enjoy the ride since the beginning of the bus line.

As they neared their destination, Bilge lapsed into one of his pouting moods, sad eyes tearing, bottom lip protruding, and all. Always in tune with her man, Betty asked, "What's the matter, my baby boy? Tell Mommy."

Bilge's bottom lip protruded a little further and his sad, sunken eyes became misty.

Betty asked again, "Come on. Come on, baby boy. Tell Mommy what's wrong."

After reducing himself to the age of a five-year-old to get his way, knowing that all men pull this crap, he said, "Betty, I'm afraid we're going to give those people at the boatyard the wrong impression."

"What do you mean, sweetie pie?"

"They are going to see us dressed all wrong and think we don't know anything about boats and take disadvantage of us. We may not know where all the parts go, but we know what the parts of the boat are and that makes us part right."

"Oh, Bilge," Betty comforted, "they wouldn't do a thing like that. I'm sure that everyone at the Sink and Sunk Boatyard is very honest. Anyway, remember that man at the bus stop who said, 'there must be at least one honest boatyard someplace.' Anyway, honey, what should we do?"

"Well, I think we should dress right. You know, dazzle them with our attire. You know what I always say, 'Dress the damn part so they won't think you're a fart.'"

"Ooooohhh, that's splendid, Bilge. You are so right. We gotta be careful especially down in Florida which is supposed to be the South but everybody from the North lives there. Why they might get the idea there is such a thing as a dumb Yankee and we don't want those people to think we are the ones who started that idea."

"Betty, you're so right about everything."

"Bilge, why don't we stay at one of those exclusive Days Inns to set up our base of operandi?"

"That's a great idea, Betty, my darling. We can work out our whole modus there. We'll get us a Wal-Mart catalog to shop in and when we're finished, there ain't no something we won't look like."

Anyway, after ten hours of rambling through five discount stores, and Bilge insisting that shopping with your wife should be listed under cruel and unusual punishment, Bilge and Betty were prepared to convince everybody at the boatyard that they were old salt shakers . . . real Number One boaty types!

When Bilge stepped forth, Betty exclaimed, "Oooooohhhhh, Bilge, you are so salty looking! That blue blazer with all those brass buttons sure looks impressive."

"Yeah Betty, sewing on those extra brass buttons really set it off . . . six to a side. I'll bet nobody else has a coat like this!"

[THANK GOD.]

"Betty, are you sure you like the white slacks and the red ascot?"

"Ooohhhh, Bilge, don't be a silly goose. With those white patent leather shoes and the captain's hat with the extra gold braid, the red ascot is a must!"

"Betty, I'm glad you bought three of those little short sun dresses, red, white, and blue. With those high heels, and that jaunty hat that says `Mate', you sure are looking up sailor!"

[SO WILL EVERY MAN IN THE BOATYARD WHEN SHE GOES UP THE LADDER.]

This wouldn't bother Bilge since he never looked up anyway. His ex-boss, Mr. Chick-In-Sheet, always told him, "You should look up, Bilge. Things always look better when you look up."

[BEING IN LADIES' UNDERWEAR, BILGE NEVER COULD UNDERSTAND WHY.]

Anyway, they arrived at The Sink and Sunk Boatyard the

next morning and immediately drew the attention and stares of everyone. One guy fell off a ladder in fright, another guy sanded the end of his finger flat, two pelicans flew into the side of a building... and if you think that ain't something... a sea gull was so shocked, it failed to crap on a freshly painted boat.

Becoming aware of the stares, Bilge whispered, "Betty, we got them fooled. Gawk, you yokels! Now you know what a real salt shaker looks like!"

The Sink and Sunk Boatyard had boats strewn about in varying order of repair. The office building, on the other hand, reminded Bilge of that old song, 'It's only a shanty in old shanty town, its roof is so slanty it touches the ground'. When the two beauties walked into the outer office, it smelled of mildew, with tired and worn furniture. The staff was so overwhelmed by their appearance that the secretary poured coffee into the palm of her hand when she failed to pick up her cup. Mr. Snook, the owner of The Sink And Sunk Boatyard, on seeing these two suckers with potential, said, "You must be the Scuppers... Lawer Potters-A-Field warned me you were coming and to be sure to look out for you."

[DON'T READ THAT STATEMENT TOO CLOSE OR YOU MAY GET THE RIGHT MEANING.]

Always ready to help, Betty said, "His name is not Lawyer. His brother-in-law is named Lawyer. The lawyer is Underwood. By the way, sir, it's so thoughtful of you to have your boatyard by the water. Your customers must really appreciate your kindness and consideration."

"Thank you, ma'am, I needed that this morning along with my IRS audit."

"You're so welcome to both, sir."

"Well, anyway, I see you folks are all dressed up and ready to take over your boat. Step into my office."

[I'M TEMPTED TO ADD "SAID THE SPIDER TO THE FLY".]

Mr Snook's office reminded one of a sex den, with every dirty calendar from the thirties-on plastered to the wall. The office reeked of musk oil and clashed with Mr. Snook's aftershave, which smelled like last week's garbage.

Bilge said, after two sneezes, "We sure are ready for our

boat, but could you tell me what happened to our Uncle Side Scuppers? I thought he was in real good shape with all that jogging and stuff like that."

"Well, sir, I don't really know what happened. He was so full of life running around that old boat getting all kinds of things done. I want you to know, sir, we did everything he needed."

From the outer office came, "And a helluva lot he didn't."

Looking over his shoulder, Mr. Snook asked, "Did you say something, Miss Dis-Con-Tent?"

The secretary, Miss Dis-Con-Tent, was wiping her coffee-stained hand and said, "Not a thing, boss, not a thing."

Mr. Snook continued, "He was the happiest man in the whole world when everything had been completed on his boat. Like the good fella he was, he came in to pay his bill and like the good fella I am, I presented it to him. A strange thing happened while he was looking at his bill. He seemed to get sick. Then he turned kinda white, then blue, then grabbed hold of the desk to keep from falling. That man started foaming at the mouth as he continued reading his bill. You could tell he thought I was fair by his tears . . . and he was a fair man, too, even though he turned blue and was foaming at the mouth. With shaky hands, the man wrote out his check. Then after a strange inquiring look at me, he walked outside. . . took one loooonnnggg look at his boat, waved goodbye . . . and dropped dead."

With tears in her eyes, Betty declared, "How romantic! It was the last look at what made him the happiest!"

"Yeah, Betty, too bad he dropped dead after paying his bill. He must have been overjoyed with happiness. Just think of how unhappy some people are! Remember that fella we passed on our way into this office? We heard him say, `The son-of-a-b%&^*$%# at the boatyard had robbed him.'"

Mr. Snook, with a monumental manure-eating look on his face said, "That happened on his way down here, poor man. There are a lot of crooks out on them there streets. You're safe here, sir. Nobody ever feels like he got robbed in a boatyard."

"Yeah," Bilge said, "I really feel safe in your hands, Mr. Snooker."

While listening to this B. S. conversation, the secretary was having a hard time holding down her breakfast.

"Well, you lucky people, everything is all paid for. She's all y'urine, you lucky sailors. Let me show you MY MISTAKE."

Bilge put on his best frown and Betty's eyes narrowed. She was squinty-eyed anyway and couldn't see half of what was going on. She claimed her glasses made her look old.

Betty stomped her foot and squinted her eyes, her most severe threat, and said, "Mr. Smucker, I thought everything was complete. I didn't know there were any mistakes."

"Oh no, ma'am, there's definitely no mistake. I just want the pleasure of showing you MY MISTAKE."

Betty got a stormy look on her face and asked, "Sir, are you ill? I thought you just said there was no mistake."

"No, ma'am, there's no mistake. It's your MISTAKE I want to show you, she..., it's MY MISTAKE."

Bilge took over, "Sir, we're not interested in your mistake or any you claim we made. We came here to see our boat."

With a trembling voice, Mr. Snook said, "That's what I'm trying to tell you, sir. Once I show you MY MISTAKE, this whole mistake will be settled."

Bilge took Betty aside and politely whispered, "Betty, let's humor this idiot. He doesn't seem to know what the hell he's talking about."

The two very understanding people returned and Bilge said, "Mr. Snickers, show us your mistake."

Feeling that he may have gotten through to these two dummies, he said, "I don't want to show you my mistake, sir, I want to show you your MY MISTAKE."

Betty stomped her foot twice, a sign of extreme anger and said with her eyes squinting and blinking, "Sir, the only mistake was my poor uncle coming to this boatyard and dying in the wrong place."

The secretary mumbled, "You can say that again, lady."

Mr. Snook asked, "You said something, Miss Dis-Con-Tent?"

"Oh, I just said, you can say that, lady ... everybody knows the boat is MY MISTAKE."

Betty would have none of that. "You don't have to take up for your boss, honey. They passed the women's suffering act a long time ago."

In a meek pleading voice, Mr. Snook asked, "Miss Dis-Con-Tent, how do I get out of this?"

She thought, you could always drop dead, you old pirate. But instead she said, "Boss, you stay here and enjoy your IRS audit. There may be more phone calls coming in because I understand that someone also reported you to the state. I'll show these nice people their boat."

Being a grateful man, Mr. Snook thought, I'm going to raise that girl's pay in three or four years.

As the two old salts walked through the boatyard, dogs barked, pelicans got diarrhea, and some of the boatyard workers started to sing, "Take this job and shove it. I ain't working here no more."

When they arrived at the stern of their boat, lo and behold there in genuine hand carved, artificial gold letters was the name of the boat, MY MISTAKE. Betty and Bilge were delightfully surprised, but their delight turned to embarrassment when they looked toward Miss Dis-Con-Tent.

Bilge regained his composure and said, "That's it . . . she, it's . . . MY MISTAKE. Betty, we're rich or we sure the hell can act like it!"

"We sure are, Bilge. We can be real phonies, not phony phonies and everybody will think we're rich because we own a boat. Bilge, Mr. Chick-In-Sheet is going to think you took a piece of everything that comes in ladies' underwear for yourself." Bilge nodded in agreement, but maintained a dumb look on his face.

[AT-A-BOY BILGE, BETTER TO LOOK DUMB THAN OPEN YOUR MOUTH AND REMOVE ALL DOUBT.]

They danced around hugging and kissing each other, experiencing one of the greatest joys in a boat owner's life. The day he gets it.

[THE OTHER JOY IS THE DAY YOU GET RID OF IT. UNLESS YOU'RE ONE OF US BLIND SUFFERERS WHO LOVE THESE FLOATING MONSTERS THAT GOBBLE UP YOUR MONEY LIKE A SESAME STREET COOKIE

MONSTER.]

Anyway, she, it, was a fifty-foot, wooden, double cabin, completely restored powerboat. She had all the equipment she needed and a helluva lot she didn't. That fair-minded crook Mr. Snook had seen to that.

Bilge, looking like a kid in a candy store, inquired meekly, "Betty, should we go on it?"

"Bilge," Betty whispered, "I don't know how."

While all this good stuff was going on between Bilge and Betty, suddenly Miss Dis-Con-Tent became a born again Christian. She now was convinced there was a God because here came the perfect opportunity for revenge.

Chief Petty Officer Cheap-Handsy was approaching the trio. She hated this dipstick with a brain of a hockey puck and the disposition of a sex maniac. But God was kind. He placed this tit pinching, know-it-all here, at this boatyard, at this precise moment in time, just for her.

"Mr. and Mrs. Scuppers, if you would like a first class tour around your boat, the right man has just arrived."

Betty said, "Oh, my, my, my. That's swwweeeeet of you, Miss Dis-Con-Tent. By the way, we didn't get your first name."

"Fully, ma'am. My mother wanted to be reminded about how she felt about my father."

Betty vocalized, "Fully Dis-Con-Tent. Oh, that's so romantic!"

Chief Cheap-Handsy approached, staring at both girls like a wild-eyed sex maniac and hungrily asked, "What can I do for you, lovely ladies?"

"Cheap, I mean Chief, I would like to introduce you to these two lovely people, Mr. Bilge Scuppers and his wife, Betty."

Addressing the Scuppers, she turned and said, "Darling people, the chief is a real know-it-all, about boats, that is."

Bilge shook hands. Betty gave a little curtsy that Bilge always thought was so genteel.

Betty stated, "We are so pleased to meet you, Mr. Chimpanzee. It's so exciting to meet a real know-it-all about boats."

Fully Dis-Con-Tent asked, "Chief, would you be kind enough to show these nice people around their boat? You're so great at such things." She knew that with a little smoke blown up this guy's ass he'd do anything.

The chief, being the modest type, said, "Well, you lucky people, you're so fortunate to have the best at your service. Why don't we go aboard?"

Betty asked, "Aboard, what board?"

The chief's smile diminished as he answered, "The boat, ma'am."

Betty looked around and under the boat and inquired, "There are boards left on the boat?"

"No, ma'am, that's how we sea dogs say, 'get on the boat'."

"Then, why don't you just say 'let's get on the boat'?"

Bilge came to his wife's rescue and said, "Betty, the chief is nautical-legalizing."

"Bilge, do you think it's safe? It looks awfully strange to me sitting on all those sticks and blocks. Why did they take it out of the water?"

Bilge gave the chief one of these, "I don't have the slightest idea," looks. It was ole Cheap-Handsy to the rescue.

"Well, pretty little lady, that's so they can work on the bottom and give it a good paint job."

Betty shook her head expressing her skepticism, "Chief, I think it would be a lot simpler to leave it in the water and hire some of those Cousteau kind of people to do what's necessary under the water. After all, those little fish must be real aggravated having cameras stuck in their faces all the time. This would give those Cousteau types something useful to do for a change."

The chief was thinking, if I answer this shit, there's no way to keep from being arrested. But, with this broad, any answer is better than nothing. So, why not give her a nothing answer?

"Well, lady, you're probably right. I'll pass that suggestion along. So, why don't we go aboard?

Anyway, being a typical woman, Betty gave the chief a "what's that crap supposed to mean" look. [SOUNDS TO ME LIKE ONE OF THOSE "SURE I LOVE YOU, HONEY,

NOW GO TO SLEEP" ANSWERS.]

Betty was willing, she started up the ladder in her short sundress and high heels. Bilge's attention was drawn to the twin screws on the boat. Cheap-Handsy was watching Betty climb up the ladder and had a different type of screw on his mind.

Once aboard, Bilge began running around like a kid on his first day at the playground. He touched and pulled on everything in sight.

Cheap-Handsy, being the type of gentleman he was, was still trying to get his eyeballs back into their sockets.

[IF THIS TYPE OF ASSHOLE IS A GENTLEMAN, JACK THE RIPPER IS A BLOODY SAINT.]

Once aboard Cheap-Handsy suggested that he show Betty around the boat. The chief, sounding like a telephone breather, announced, "Well, little lady, I'm going to teach you the directions aboard a boat. That way is forward or ahead," the chief smiled while pointing to the front of the boat with his left hand. "That way, is aft or the stern," he added with his right hand, directing Betty's attention to the back of the boat.

Betty nodded her head in agreement. That didn't necessarily mean she understood. It was a nervous habit of hers when she only got half of what was going on.

"Now, little lady, I'm going to show you the necessary comforts aboard the vessel." The chief gave a risque wink and added, "If you know what I mean."

Betty replied with a blank look, "I don't."

"Well, don't worry, little lady. You're in good hands with ole' Cheap-Handsy, ha .. ha. Well, anyway, ma'am, let's go below."

"Below what, sir?"

"The decks, ma'am."

"Decks of what?"

"The boat, ma'am. You're standing on them."

Betty lifted her foot to see what she was standing on. The chief explained that the floor on the boat was called the deck. Here it comes ... Betty asked, "Why?"

The chief looked up to the big Coast Guard Cutter In The Sky, asked for forgiveness for his answer, and replied, "Because there's a whole stack of them on a boat."

[NOW, THIS WAS SOMETHING BETTY COULD HANDLE.]

Betty followed the chief down below. The chief said, "I'm going to show you a head." He started for the back of the boat.

And in a squeaky polite voice, Betty said, "Sir, I think you're going in the wrong direction."

"No, I'm not, little lady. I said I was going to show you a head."

"Sir, you distinctly pointed out to me that that direction is the back of the boat."

"I know it is the back of the boat, lady, but that is where a head is."

Betty said, "Mr. Cheap Cheap, if you're lost, sir, just say so. I'll understand."

Cheap-Handsy started to turn a little blue around the mouth and declared, "Lady, I never get lost on a boat. I know where a head is and it's astern."

Betty scolded, "Sir, are you deliberately trying to take disadvantage of me because I'm a lady?"

"Ma'am, if you don't want to see a head that is astern, I will show you a head that is ahead." This old Coast Guard pain-in-the-ass was thinking that maybe it was time to take up chicken farming in Kansas.

"Ma'am, if we go to a head which I assure you is astern, you will plainly see that a head is in the back of the boat." The chief was starting to foam at the mouth.

Betty's eyes squinted and she threatened, "I double, double dare you."

The chief stormed off down the passageway towards the stern. At the first door he came to, he flung it open and declared, "There it is, lady doubter. A head... A Crapper, if you will... And a potty, if you must. Ha! Ha! and Ha!"

Betty stomped her foot in defiance and declared, "You are a big fibber. Anyone can see that's a bathroom."

The chief, turning various shades of red and purple, staggered topside. Enough of this damn broad was enough. He changed his mind, returned below and quipped, "Not only that, Miss Smarty Pants, if you want to see a head that is ahead,

I'll show you a head that's ahead. There are two heads on this boat"

Betty quipped, "I hope you are not including yours as one that has brains."

Betty felt contented that she had exposed this phony. She decided while she was there she might as well use the potty. After all, the smart-alec did say, "If you must, you must". And, she politely gave the chief a kiss-off look and slammed the door in his face.

The chief thought, just like all women, this broad must tinkle every hour on the hour. "Oh, NO!" He started beating frantically on the door and yelled, "Don't do it! Don't do it! Not in the boatyard!"

Betty squealed, "Get away from the door, you perverter. A lady can't tee tee with someone listening."

Fog set in in the chief's brain as he staggered topside in hopeless defeat.

Anyway, with nature's pressure relieved, it was time to flush. Betty looked around diligently, oh, my God, where's the handle? Oh, my God, there's no, handle! How embarrassing! With her frustration and embarrassment mounting, Betty whimpered, "What do I do now? I know. I'll go ask Bilge. He'll know what to do."

Betty should have consulted an empty book. Her genius was trying to get all the little green dots and lines out of the radar set so the picture would be at least as good as his TV set at home.

After running wildly around the boat, she finally heard Bilge raising hell upstairs. Betty entered the flying bridge and Bilge fumed, "Look at this picture. The whole thing is full of dots and squiggly lines! How in the hell am I supposed to know where we are?"

"If you want to know where we are, darling, why don't you ask someone? Besides, darling boy, Mommy's got a bigger problem. Someone stole the handle off the potty and Mommy made tee tee."

"Don't worry, honey, I'll ask Chief Know-It-All. That smart ass should be good for something."

The chief was hanging over the side looking for his marbles.

He was sure he lost them somewhere around this boat.

Bilge slipped up quietly to the chief and whispered, "Chief, we have a small problem. My wife used the potty and someone stole the handle."

The chief snapped, "There's no handle, sir."

"That's what I just said, Chief. Someone stole the handle."

"Sir, no one stole the bloody thing. There is no damn handle."

Bilge quipped, "Sir, I don't give a damn if it snuck away during the night on a magic carpet. There's no handle and my wife filled the potty with tee tee and I would like to flush it."

The chief exploded, "Listen, boot, I mean, sir. First, there is no handle. Second, the handle on a boat is a damn button. And third, you can't flush it in a boatyard because there's no place for it to go. So, therefore, I'm leaving this floating insane asylum with whatever shred of sanity you two nuts have left me." After mustering his remaining dignity, the chief shot the bird at the boat's ensign and left.

Bilge was completely disgusted with that spoiled sport and yelled at the departing chief, "If you fall off the ladder make sure it's not on something we need." Then he returned to his sweet wife, saying, "Betty, it's not a handle. It's a button."

Betty went down below in a flash. Bilge's brain made two revolutions before he realized that he failed to tell her not to flush in the boatyard. He immediately knew it was too late by the screams and curses coming from the chief. The chief had taken a shortcut under the boat and was at the right time in the wrong place. Never was a man so pissed off from being pissed on and deserving it more.

Anyway, the fully contented, Miss Fully Dis-Con-Tent, after hearing the screams of the pissed on, pissed off, Chief Cheap-Handsy and the cheers from the yard men, came aboard and said, "I know you sweet people would like to know more about your boat... not that you don't already know a lot about boats." [ONLY A VENGEFUL WOMAN CAN LIE WITH A STRAIGHT FACE AT A TIME LIKE THIS.]

She continued, "I think you both should take some Coast Guard and Power Squadron classes. It's really a lot of fun."

Miss Dis-Con-Tent, being a devious, conniving and vengeful woman, decided to get even with one more lover boy.

It seems a certain lover boy invited her on a Dutch treat date and instead of saying, "Your place or mine?" he asked, "Would you like to pay for the hotel room?" Thank God the cheapskate had suggested using her car so the jerk could save his own gas. She was grateful they were well out of town and it was raining like hell when the cheap son-of-a-b$%&$#&$* popped the question. He had a long wet walk home. She knew this was the lover who taught the Power Squadron classes.

Bilge expressed his joy, "Why, that's sweet of you to suggest those classes, Miss Fuller Whatever! We will be nautical-legalizing with the best."

Sheepishly she answered, "Why, sir, that's what all that B.S. talk they teach you is about."

"You hear that, Betty? B.S., on the waterway means boats and ships. We're learning how to talk it already."

Betty asked, "Miss Fully Malcontent, do you think the instructors will allow us to take the classes even though we don't own a car."

Bilge added, "I don't even have a license."

"It doesn't matter that you don't have a license, Mrs. Scuppers. Very few people have licenses to operate their boats. I'll gladly make all the arrangements for you to attend the classes tonight. By the way, Mr. Scuppers, the boss wanted me to remind you that we're going to launch your boat tomorrow."

## NAVIGATION LIGHTS

Recreational vessels are required to display navigation lights between sunset and sunrise and other periods of reduced visibility (fog, rain, haze etc.). The U. S. Coast Guard Navigation Rules, International - Inland encompasses lighting requirements for every description of watercraft. The information provided here is intended for power-driven and sailing vessels less than 20 meters.

### POWER DRIVEN VESSELS

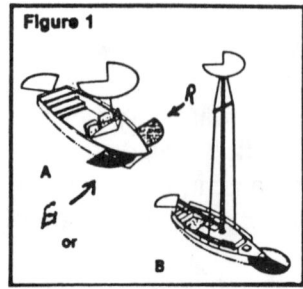
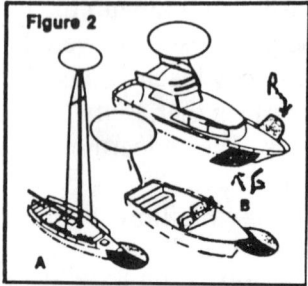

**Sailing Vessels and Vessels Under Oars**

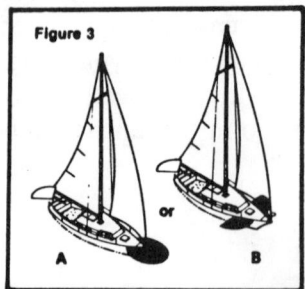
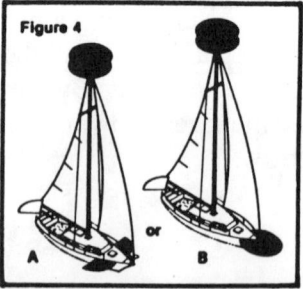

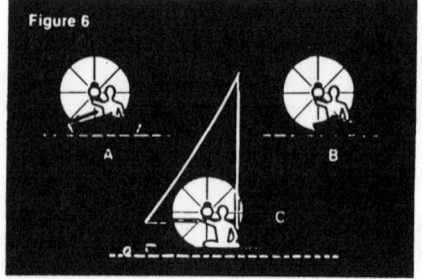

# CHAPTER THREE

That evening Betty and Bilge were introduced at the Power Squadron class along with all the other new students. Lieutenant Blowhard realized immediately that the Scuppers were new boat owners. They quickly identified themselves by asking a lot of dumb questions. He singled out Betty as the prototype he wanted to use for the course demonstrations. He didn't think he could handle Bilge wearing that loud blue blazer in front of the class. Anyway, he thought, I would look a lot better in that jacket than he does. But I wouldn't dare, it would force me to come out of the closet and declare my sexual preference. And, the government does frown on the strangest things.

Lyrically he announced, "In tonight's class, ladies and gentlemen, we're going to review the directions aboard a boat. To make matters simple, I'm going to draw the deck of a very large boat on the blackboard. Mrs. Scuppers has graciously agreed to act as our captain this evening. Mrs. Scuppers, would you kindly stand and face the blackboard directly in front of the boat?"

Betty readily agreed after giving the class a cute curtsy.

Lieutenant Blowhard said, "Captain Betty, please place your left hand on the port side and your right hand on the starboard side."

Betty asked, "Port side of what? And the starboard side of who?"

"Mrs. Scuppers, your starboard side is at your right hand facing forward and your port side is at your left hand."

"Lieutenant, do you and Chief Cheap-Handsy belong to the same Coast Guard?"

"Why yes, ma'am. Why do you ask?"

"Well, today, sir, aboard our boat, the chief distinctly told me and insisted, as he was standing on our deck and pointing with his left hand to the front, that it was the bow of the boat. With his right hand he pointed and said that was the stern of the boat." She giggled a little and continued, "That's where a head is."

"Ma'am, there must be some mistake. Why don't you disregard what the chief said and I'll see if I can clarify this for you. As you're looking toward the blackboard, point with your left hand to your port side. So you'll remember this easily, port wine is red and, by the way, that's the side with the red light. The starboard side, where you're pointing your right hand, is the green side and has a green light."

Betty asked for clarification. "Lieutenant Blowup, what kind of wine is the green light made of?"

The lieutenant, a little befuddled, said, "I don't know what kind of wine is green, ma'am. I would like to make one thing perfectly clear before we go any further . . . ahead is not astern."

"Then, sir, as I suspected when the chief attempted to tell me that by going astern, he would show me a head, he really showed me a potty. As I suspected the poor man didn't have any idea what he was talking about."

"Oh, I understand, ma'am. That's right. It's my mistake."

"NO, sir! Betty quickly corrected, She, ... it's MY MIS-TAKE."

"Lady, pleeeaaassssse . . . control yourself."

Betty stomped her foot and demanded, "So, I'm asking you, sir, what's right and who is wrong? You say, a head is astern - your port light is made of red wine - your left hand is a head, and your right hand is astern which is really a green light and doesn't have any wine in it? I'm afraid you're getting confused, sir, or you're trying to confuse us by over nautical-legalizing."

Anyway, the whole class applauded.

[THIS MUST HAVE BEEN DUMMY NIGHT AT THE OLD POWER SQUADRON. I MUST CONFESS I ONCE TRIED TO TEACH ON A NIGHT LIKE THIS.]

Lieutenant Blowhard was still trying to unravel the previous statement. He attempted to compare the lady's statement to something relevant and the only thing his brain could come up with was his income tax form.

Getting close to a nervous breakdown, the lieutenant stated, "Ma'am, let's see if we can unravel this Gordean knot." The lieutenant was thinking that it may take a Greek sword to chop through this broad's head. Wiping his brow he remarked, "I think the chief was trying to explain one thing to you and I'm attempting to explain another."

"I understand that, sir, but which one of you is right, if any? And, for heaven's sake why are you trying to teach us knots, when we don't know what type of wine the port green side is? It's just a simple thing, I would like to know what's right, if who? "

[MORE APPLAUSE FROM THE BUNCH OF DUMMIES IN THE CLASS.]

With a deep sigh, Blowhard, placed his hands on his hips and snickered, "We're both right, ma'am."

"Ridiculous, sir, ridiculous, only a female can make a right out of two wrongs."

Lieutenant Blowhard was thinking, if she only knew. Anyway, if I'm smart enough to get money from my mom and dad at age forty-five, I should be able to handle this situation. "Mrs. Scuppers, let's take a totally new approach. We'll assume that ahead is ahead and astern is astern. We'll totally disregard any left or right hand directions given by the chief. Now, point your left hand out toward the port side of the boat . . . point your right hand out toward the starboard side of the boat . . . and now, you are facing ahead."

"Is that the same thing as the potty?"

The lieutenant mumbled to himself, "How the hell did I get into this?

"A head is a potty, ma'am, to use a landlubber's term. Ahead is also ahead, you know, when you're going ahead."

"That's very polite of you, sir. That's exactly what I have to do. I'll be back in a moment."

Someone must have blown the bugle for a cavalry charge, every lady in the audience left with her. [FAR BE IT FOR ONE OF THEM TO GO TO THE BATHROOM ALONE. THIS WOULD SET A VERY DANGEROUS PRECEDENT.] When the ladies returned with looks of relief on their faces, he proceeded. "Now, class," of idiots, he thought, "I think we are finally making some real progress."

Bilge was scratching his head while thinking, what progress? I don't see any progress and I'm taking notes. This guy is making about as much progress as a politician's promise.

Blowhard surrendered, "Anyway, class, we have determined that a head is the same as a potty."

At that moment Commander May Day entered the room.

[HE'S THE GUY WHO'S WRITING THE LIEUTENANT'S FITNESS REPORT.]

He was informed by none other than Miss Dis-Con-Tent that he should attend this class and look out for the best interest of the service.

Lieutenant Blowhard continued, "Okay, now, a head is the same as a potty. We've established that. Next, ahead is the direction we can go if we are astern and want to go to a potty which is a head in the front of the boat."

Commander May Day was thinking, this fitness report will either show that the lieutenant is an idiot or it will be a lengthy dissertation on the decline of mental poise and intelligence in the service.

Lieutenant Blowhard's last explanation blew all the circuits in Bilge's brain, but Betty got it. He was finally talking her language.

"Now, Mrs. Scuppers, as you are facing the front of the boat which is ahead or forward, your left side is your port side. Port, left, red. Remember this, class. On your right side is your starboard side, green light. Now you understand that, don't you?"

Betty was nodding her head.

[YOU KNOW WHAT THAT MEANS, FOLKS!]

The lieutenant was thanking the great big Coast Guard Gutter In The Sky. He knew he had overcome the situation. It simply required superior intellect to handle these idiots.

After a little applause and a curtsy, Betty walked to the back of the class where Bilge was waiting. They began to whisper to each other in deep concern. Commander May Day walked pontifically to the front of the class to answer any further questions. [POOR MAN.]

Bilge raised his hand and asked, "Sir, my name is Bilge Scuppers, spelled with two pees. What we would like to know is, what kind of license is necessary to drive our boat?"

A pale ghostly look came over the commander's face. He half-coughed and half-whispered in embarrassment, "None."

"Would you speak up, sir? We didn't hear you."

"I said none. You don't need a license at all."

The room was filled with sighs of relief and disbelief. Bilge felt relieved that he didn't need a license but he wondered whether such a dumb statement could be true. When it came to dumb statements, Bilge wanted to know more.

"Sir, I am only asking this to get it straight. Are you saying that my wife, who failed her driver's test three times from no fault of her own, of course, can drive our fifty-foot, forty-ton, seven hundred horsepower boat anywhere without a license of any kind and without any experience at all? Why, sir, that's just great! But kinda stupid."

Commander May Day thought, this is sad, but true. He said, "Mr. Scuppers, you only need a license if you're going to use your boat commercially. Unfortunately, sir, even an idiot can drive his own boat without a license."

With no further questions the class was dismissed. As everybody started to leave, Betty let out a loud "meeeooowww hooooo." [SHE SOUNDED LIKE A CAT ON A BACK FENCE IN THE SUMMERTIME.]

"Meeeooowww hooooo." Everyone came to a halt.

Commander May Day, half frightened out of his skin, asked, "What's wrong, little lady?"

"That mean old man who was teaching the class told us what happens when we're facing the front of the boat and what color wine we have and don't have. But he didn't tell us what happens when we are facing the back of the boat and what color the wine becomes? If he doesn't tell us, how do we know which is port from starboard when we are going to the potty in the back of the boat?"

At this point, the commander decided that the only safe boating left was in Death Valley.

"Lady, nothing happens when you face the back of the boat. The directions toward the bow and stern remain the same. Port and starboard don't change, either."

"Oh, no, sir! I distinctly understood that my left becomes my right and my green wine becomes red. Doesn't it or what?"

"Ma'am, let's do this. Please disregard everything the lieutenant said."

"Sir, that will be easy since he didn't make any sense anyway."

More applause from the rest of the brain surgeons in the class.

"Also, sir, are you our last hope or is there a bigger disregarder than you?"

With a shaky finger, Commander May Day pointed to himself and said, "Lady, I'm the last person any of my people want to tell you to disregard."

"Oh, that's so romantic, sir. Now, what happens when I face the back of the boat?"

"Let me put it this way, the port side of the boat remains the same no matter which way you're facing. There is no wine, just a little red glass with a little light in it to make it shine red."

The area commander just entered. He was a helluva lot bigger disregarder than Commander May Day!

Commander May Day continued, "Now ain't that nice? On the starboard side which is always the starboard side, there is a little cute green glass with a pretty little light to make it shine. Guess what color, class?"

The nautical Einsteins all yelled, "GREEN."

"That's right, class. Now you're getting it. We don't want to overwhelm you with complications on your first night. We, in the Coast Guard, figure if you can tell one side of the boat from the other, I mean the port side from the starboard side, we've come a long way with any group. And you're much further advanced than most of them out there."

Lots of applause was given at the end of the class. He thought he must have screwed up somewhere because some of these people were starting to understand.

However, when wine was mentioned it jump-started the commander's brain and he headed for the nearest bar.

---

Anyway, on entering the boatyard the following morning Betty let out a hellacious scream, "Youuuuuuuuuuuuu-weeeeeeeeeeee, Bilge, some big machine has got our boat and is running away with it! Catch it! Catch it!"

Bilge increased the speed in the rented car to twenty miles an hour. That was the same speed he drove on the freeway. [YOU KNOW THE TYPE, THE ONE AT THE HEAD OF THE LINE AT RUSH HOUR.] He jumped out of the car like a TV cop, then dashed to his boat and demanded, "What the hell is going on? Where are you taking my boat?"

The gristly old driver of the lift machine answered, "We's a puttin' hers in the waters."

"What are you doing that for?"

"She, it floats betters that ways, lubber."

Betty felt like a mother whose six year old was going on stage for the first time as she watched her boat go into the water. She pleaded teary-eyed and all for everyone to be careful. With lots of sniffles, Betty cried, "Oh, Bilge, it looks so frightened and lonely out there in that big bad water."

"Don't worry, Mommy. We will take care of our MY MISTAKE. After all, she will have all our love and boating experiences to rely on."

"Mr. and Mrs. Scuppers!"

"Oh, hi, Miss Fully Disco. You were so much help getting us into that class last night. Thanks a whole bunch with sugar on top."

"Oh, that's all right, it was my pleasure. I have you set for another class, we'll all enjoy it, BELIEVE ME. By the way, there's a man in this boatyard who could really further your education. Mr. Snook volunteered his services to help get you on your way, because he likes people like you."

Miss Dis-Con-Tent was thinking what the boss really said was, "With those two out there on the water, the accident average should jump by fifty percent." With a sigh of certainty, he added, "thereby increasing our job security."

The volunteered volunteer came over. He was the same guy that was driving the boat lift.

"Mr. and Mrs. Scuppers, this is old Captain Ragg Bagger."

Captain Ragg Bagger was five feet tall with a long pony

tail hanging out of his sailor's hat. He sported a dirty gray beard and wore a blue and white striped shirt, bell-bottom pants and smoked a pipe . . . What else? Noticeable was the hair protruding out of his big ears which seemed equal to the length of his beard.

Betty cooed, "We are pleased to meet you, Captain Bag of Rags."

"Almost the same here's. Weeeeelll as you can see, Captain Bilge . . .," Bilge almost had an orgasm at being called captain for the first time. "The boss, that cream puff jerk, had me put your boat ways out on the end of the quays. Somethin' bout's his unpaids insurance."

"Bilge, it looks so lonely way out there by itself with no other boats to play with."

"Don't worry, Betty. She, it has us to play with and that should make her happy."

Ragg Bagger shuffled toward MY MISTAKE, "Wells, why's don't us go overs and get started abouts learning?"

Betty asked, "Sir, do you always put s's on everything?"

"No lady, onlys whens I talks, cans writes withouts thems."

Our two heroes followed ole Ragg Bagger aboard their boat like faithful little ducks. Betty pranced up the gangway, Bilge held onto the railing for dear life.

"Why don't we starts at the front of the boat which in this case is called the pulpits. It's on the bowels of the boat."

"Sir, which one of the three is it?"

"All three, lady. Just in this case theys builts this contraption to make it easier for you to drops your hooks."

Bilge said, "Sir, it looks like an anchor."

"You could calls it an anchor or you could calls it the hooks. Or you can calls it a danforth. You can calls it all them things and still be rights. But an anchors is strange animals. See, in my days, we used to consider an anchors our only hopes in desperate situations. But nows days, these new kids consider it the only ways there is to save moneys on dockage."

Anyway, Betty was taking notes as quickly as she could. She decided that everything in boating came under multiple choice answers. She showed this notation to the men. Bilge thought she was right and Old Ragg Bagger said he wasn't sure that she was wrong.

"Now the firsts thing you have to remembers about anchoring, is that anchoring is the first thing you do's when you can't figures out what else to do." Betty got that one. "Second, is makes sure you got ones and be damn sures you tie it on to somethin' before you's throws it overboard."

Bilge shook his head and said, "No one could be that dumb."

"You wants to bets, mister? More damn lies is tolds about why peoples buys new anchors than anythin' else. Next thing to remember is always anchor in a safe spot. Someplace where you are sure there is plenty of waters."

Betty said, "That's great! There's a whole bay full of it out there so we could anchor any place."

"Tain't whats I mean, lady. By plenty of waters I mean how deeps it is."

Betty took note that plenty also means deeps. You don't have to have much plenties to have plenty as long as it's plenty deeps enough!!! Or something like that.

"Nows don't ya'lls go anchoring close ups to anybody elses. There's a plenty of rooms outs there. When its comes to anchoring, peoples is likes chickens when they go to roost. They perch rights on tops of each others. Winds comes along and blows them suckers rights on top each and others boats. Then there they is, outs there in the middles of the nights in their drawers running rounds with fenders in their hands like a dog looking for a place to poops. Why, lady, I's a seen 'em with the wholes north ends of Lakes Worth to anchor in and them piles ups togethers likes cows poo in a barn."

"Sir, now that we know everything about anchoring, how do we get it into the water?"

"Wells, ya'lls knowing everything about anchoring already is fantastic, but in ya'lls case, it's kinda difficult. You see ups on thats flying bridge there's a button thats says, `anchor downs and anchor ups'. Hows that'er grab you?"

Bilge said, "I think with some practice and especially if it comes with some instructions we can work it out. Don't you think so, Betty?"

Betty nodded her head again and asked, "Mr. Frag Bag, why does the boat have a railing all the way around?"

"Firsts thing, lady, it's for looks. Then just maybes, it might keeps some drunken guests from falling overboards. Not the kids, they either falls over it or they goes under it. But I's thinks its the dogs that falls overboards the best and the mostest."

"The rails are so shiny and pretty, Betty. I think we'll keep them."

"Shines the hells out of them, mister, and theys gonna stays like thats."

"Sir, what are the floors made out of?"

The hair raised up on the back of old Ragg Bagger's neck. Fluttering his beard back and forth in indignation, he said, "Dem's aints floors, lubber, dem's decks. Floors is in houses . . . dis ain't no dang house."

"Oh, my, my, I know all about decks. Chief Chimpanzee told me they got their name by sailors playing cards and when they ran out of cards they used the ones on the boat and that's how they got their name decks and that's . . . ."

"That's fantastic, lady. Old Chief Monkey's Ass woulds tells you just anythings. Anyways, your decks is made of teaks, mostest pretty wood in the worlds, nicest wood that ever worked a man's ass off to keeps that ways."

"Mr. Raggy-Baggs, is there something special we should know about teaks?"

"Ya'lls buys yourselfs a can of teaks oils and them smart asses who makes that stuffs will tells ya'll everythings."

"Oh, sir, we don't intend spending any money just because we own a boat."

"Nows that's reallys fantastic, lady."

"Not only that, my husband intends to write a book on HOW TO OWN A BOAT AND NOT SPEND ANY MONEY."

"That's fantastic too, lady. I'll buys the first copy."

Bilge asked, "Sir why do you always say, 'that's fantastic' to everything my wife says?"

"Wells, Mr. Scuppers, it's lots politer than saying, THAT'S BULL SHIT, now ain'ts it?"

Old Ragg Bagger spent a lot of time with the Scuppers, one

whole week to be exact. Then after a long drunk he decided to quit the boat business and become what his wife had always wanted him to be. . . a bag boy at Publix.

When Betty found out, she said, "Now he's a Raggy Baggy Baggy Boy. Oh, Bilge, How romantic!"

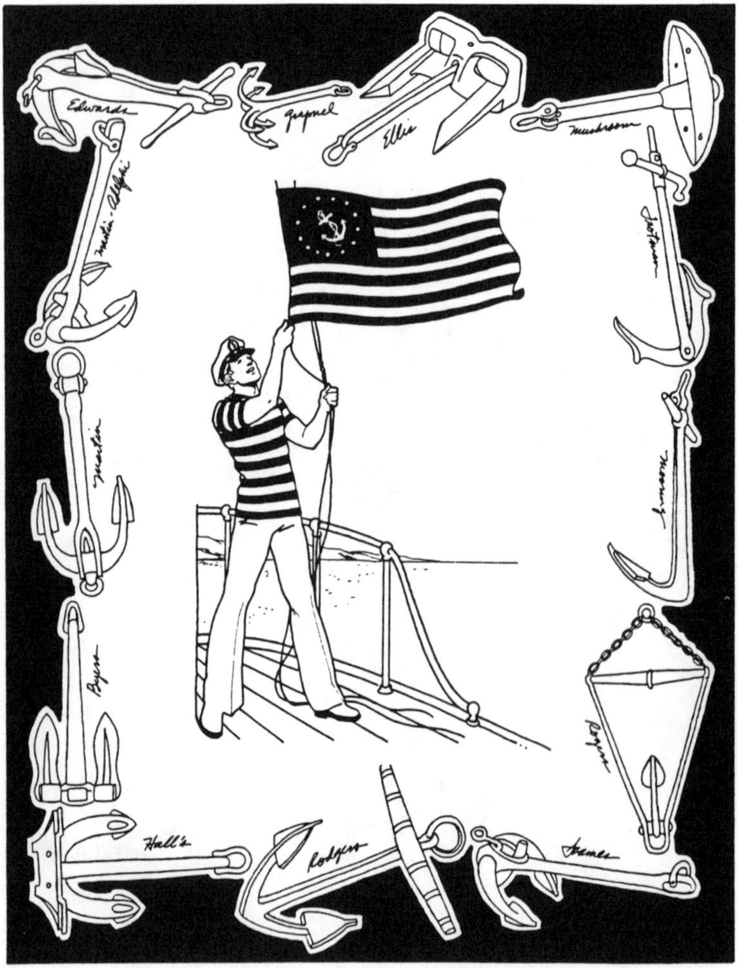

# CHAPTER FOUR

All the next week our heroes occupied their time moving their possessions aboard MY MISTAKE. They were able to bring aboard with little difficulty the things that Bilge had brought. It soon became apparent that either the boat would have to be doubled in length or Betty would have to sacrifice several of the necessities that she had brought, such as: a chandelier, four boxes of old personal records, six large stuffed animals, two boxes of porcelain dolls, three lamps with barroom type shades, three ceiling fans, her entire collection of pop-up can tops and enough clothes to stock the Salvation Army for a year. With heartbreak and tears Betty placed in storage all of those priceless possessions plus five suitcases of clothes.

Spending the first night on board was so exciting it took Betty almost one minute to fall asleep. Bilge, the brave warrior type, never did get to sleep. Each time the boat rocked or bumped the dock he was ready to abandon ship. It took our brave hero a week to get over this.

BETTY LOVED THE BOAT. SHE LOVED EVERYTHING ABOUT IT. When other boats passed by, causing MY MISTAKE to rock, you could hear her swoon, "Oh, Bilge, how romantic it is living on the sea!"

Bilge recovered from his seasickness at the dock. After all those years in ladies' underwear he was starting to look up and it helped.

The two old salt shakers were anticipating another wonderful exciting evening of nautical-legalizing instructions. Bilge decided that a blue ascot would be the ideal thing to dress down his appearance for the Power Squadron class. After changing clothes for the fourth time, Betty settled on a red sundress, a blue sun visor and a pair of white high heels, with pearls of course.

Anyway, upon arriving at the Power Squadron class they were greeted by the evening's guest speaker, Mr. Long-Winded. His previous experience, before becoming one-eighth owner of a twenty-five foot sailboat, consisted of twenty years in the Navy as a shore patrol clerk. [SHOULD ANYTHING MORE BE SAID?]

He swaggered to the front of the class, picked up the mike with a flourish and after a series of screeches and whines he announced at top volume, "Okay sailors, listen up! You women pay attention, too! You may accidentally become sailors, some day! I'm glad I removed myself from the service when they allowed women aboard ships for anything but a little bed fun. Aaah, guys!"

"Who's this asshole!" were the whispers of every lady in the audience.

"First, I'm going to give you guys some simple instructions about the IC Waterway. That's Intracoastal to you, boots. The IC Waterway on the charts is represented by yellow stripes, proceeding from Norfolk, Virginia, to Key West, Florida, but not always. Aids with red reflectors are on the starboard side; aids with green reflectors are on the port side."

[THERE WERE LOTS OF CIRCUITS BURNED IN THE BRAINS OF THE AUDIENCE AT THIS POINT.]

Betty raised her hand meekly and asked, "Sir, are you another disregarder?"

"What the hell's that supposed to mean, lady?"

"Well, sir, isn't the port the red side and the green the starboard side?"

"That's correct, lady, but not on the waterway. It's on your damn boat. Red is on your port side if you're heading north, but red is on your green side if you're heading south. But not if you're heading east and west. Pay attention! This is very simple! Where the Intracoastal joins with other waterways, dual purpose aids are provided which you'll find are very distinctive on your chart. Yellow triangles are located on your starboard side and yellow squares are located on your port side."

Bilge asked, "Sir, are all these colors the same on the chart as they are on the waterway?"

"Definitely not, what's wrong with you, fellow, do you expect our government to be consistent? Pay attention, sir. I'll make this simple. Now, I know a few of you experienced ones understand this and it would be a damn miracle if you first-timers understood it at all." The whole class was nodding their heads.

"Now I hope you all understood my previous explanation. Let's go on and discuss the further information that is provided on your charts. The depth of the water is very important. You will find that the depth of the water from Norfolk, Virginia, to Fort Pierce, Florida, is twelve feet and from Fort Pierce to Miami is ten feet and from Miami to Florida Bay is seven feet. The Coast Guard publishes local notices to mariners because these depths vary continuously. Now understand something. In nautical terms the depth of the water is always referred to in fathoms. A fathom is six feet of water. But in the Intracoastal Waterway from Norfolk to wherever, the depth is given in feet. Now many of us who have been around a long time call the ICW the Ditch. Well, the Ditch doesn't stretch from Norfolk to Florida Bay...as I said, it goes from Key West, Florida, to Cape Ann, Massachusetts, or you could say from the Dry Tortugas all the way to Maine on other government charts. Then, of course, there's that other little eight or nine hundred mile part from Florida to Corpus Christi, Texas."

"Sir, my name is Mr. Hate-Full and I'm a retired IRS agent."

A chorus of boos was issued from the class.

"Sir, what I was saying before I was cheered was that my job at the IRS was to make income tax forms confusing. I just want to mention, sir, though I understood most of the confusion that I caused, I don't understand any of this shit."

"That makes us even, doesn't it, Mr. Hate-Full. I don't understand your damn income tax forms, either." The audience applauded and yelled that the score was now at deuce.

"Getting back to being polite, class... you might meet just about any type of vessel on these waterways. Mr. Hate-Full, before you ask what kind of vessels you can expect on the waterway you will find any type from little runabouts to big ole ships. But normally, you'll meet sailboats that have a habit of getting in the way. Then there are the trawlers, mostly owned by Yankees, but they don't trawl for anything. They've got this thing about owning deep sea boats even though they never travel there. You'll find that they travel around eight to ten knots on the waterway, leave late in the morning and stop early in the evening to drink, I mean rest.

"Of course, there's the Palm Beach and Coral Gables elite, the normal folks in their sixty-foot little ole million dollar jobbies, who travel around twenty-five knots and wash everybody's ass out of the channel as they pass. Then there's the occasional local dope organization traveling around eighty knots. Pursued by the Coast Guard in their boats going twenty knots. Then there's the DEA, the Drug Enforcement Agency, chasing everybody down, if they can bum a ride, that is.

"Why, not too long ago those boys in hot pursuit captured a boat worth five million dollars that was tied to the dock with three dollars worth of marijuana on it and they seized the whole damn thing. Now, those boys have in mind real government values in pursuit. And then, you might meet the southbound migration of the snowbirds. Normally you meet them in the fall running from the cold weather that they love to talk about. And you're really lucky if you meet one of these birds up North. The first damn thing these northern snowbirds do when they buy a boat, is haul ass to Florida."

Betty whispered in Bilge's ear, "Now I know how those birdies and duckies find their way back and forth. They just follow all those buoys on the wrong side of the water."

Bilge whispered back, "Yeah, Betty darling. If we aren't careful we might learn something in this class."

Mr. Longwinded continued, "I know you first timers, better known as boots, will have a lot of questions — extremely intelligent questions. One I'm usually plagued with is, will I run aground? That's an absolute maybe, folks. You just stay between the red and green markers and you'll always be safe. I've even been asked whether a waterway trip is boring. Shucks, I've made the trip allllll the way from the north end of Lake Worth, way down to Fort Lauderdale, about fifty miles, and I've never been bored yet.

"I must admit we did run aground three times on our first run but that's because our boat draws three feet of water. Then there's the other question, how difficult is it to follow the charts? That's the silliest of all questions. Listen to how simple the explanations are tonight. It's as simple to follow those charts as it is to follow my lecture. But I'm sure the ladies are missing the whole thing."

There were whispers from the back of the class – "Big asshole with ears."

The guy on the other side of Bilge leaned over and said, "Ole buddy, if his lecture is simple, I think we're in some deep trouble!"

At this point, a very polite little old lady in the front of the class stood up and said, "Sir, I'm sure Longwinded is your first name, because I'm convinced that Idiot is your last name. GOOD NIGHT."

After a few forced grins, Longwinded said, "The lady leaving was not destined to be a great seagoing mariner."

One could hear whispers of feminine voices, saying, "Idiot he is and Idiot he will always be."

The instructor continued, "One thing, boots, plan your trips. Study your charts and remember, the Ditch is a free trip. There are no tolls and no costs for traveling on the waterway."

Bilge said, "You see, Betty, I told you it doesn't cost anything to travel on a boat."

"Some folks like to make extensive planning. Mark out your destinations on your chart. It helps to know where you're going. The next consideration, of course, is the reason for your chart and that is to know where you are at all times.

"Now, let's talk about traveling on the waterway and on which side you should travel. When you meet an oncoming vessel, it is always best to direct your course to the starboard, which in some cases would be the port side of the channel, but not always. I mean a channel that is coming in from the sea is the port side. The red markers are on the port side; also coming in from the sea. So if you are coming in from the sea and you meet a vessel traveling outbound, you steer to your starboard which is the port side of the channel. The outbound vessel will do the same.

"What are you asking, boot? No damn it, not your same side but his same side. So, to make things even simpler, if you direct your course to the starboard and he directs his course to the starboard, then you will pass port to port. Or even simpler, you will direct your course to the one whistle side and pass two whistles to two whistles. Now that's simple, isn't it?"

Talk about some brain surgeons needing surgery, they're here in this class.

[THE INSTRUCTOR'S STATEMENT IS CORRECT.] FROM THE FEDERAL REQUIREMENTS AND SAFETY TIPS FOR RECREATIONAL BOATERS: Mariners must NOT rely on buoys alone for determining their position. Storms and wave action can cause buoys to move. [WHAT THE HELL ARE WE SUPPOSED TO RELY ON?!]

Betty rose, notes in hand and questioned, "Sir, am I supposed to whistle or is my husband? And is that to be done out of the window or on the radio?"

Longwinded rolled his eyes up in the air and said, "Lady, those are all nautical terms used by towboat people and us experienced sailors."

More whispers of "the hell with him" came from the class.

The lady on the side of Betty whispered, "Don't worry Betty, you don't have to know the first thing about driving a boat or worry about needing a license. There's no law to stop you. Just get in and go. People poke a little fun at the Coast Guard, but if it wasn't for those guys there would be slaughter on the water."

Betty said, "Oh, that's so romantic."

Longwinded continued, "Now that we fully understand how to pass each other on the waterway . . ."

The fella on the side of Bilge stood up and interrupted, "Sir, what happens when we meet one of those big towboats with lots of barges?"

"I'm glad you asked that question. Most of these gentlemen are the knights of the waterway and have many years of experience. Even with their huge towboats and monstrous tows which take up most of the channel, they are very easy to get along with. They know all the rules of piloting and are licensed captains. My advice to you is to give them the whole damn waterway or one of those polite knights of the waterway might just up and run over your ass.

"Have I oversimplified this? If I did, look at it this way,

pleasure boaters. Think of a towboat with a string of barges representing ten eighteen-wheelers tied together coming down the interstate with no brakes. When he blows his horn, it means move your ass or it's going to be grass. It may come as a startling surprise, boots, but there are no brake pedals on a boat. You either back the damn thing down, dodge real fast, or run like hell."

The questioner became one pale sick sucker and nervously resumed his seat.

"Anyway, it will be exciting to encounter many different types of bridges and boats along the waterway. Some bridge tenders seem, in my opinion, to come from one particular group of humanity that always seems to be aggravated. The type that becomes bridge tenders are the meanest, most cantankerous, stubborn, uncooperative state employees and they are selected because they hate pleasure boaters. Now ya'll stop that whispering in the audience about state employees. They're not all slow and aggravating people. You see, I met one about twenty-two years ago who was nice. It surprised me so much that I did her the favor of marrying her. What's that talk going on back there? You say someone took a couple of shots and threw bricks at the bridge tender at Stickney Point. So, what's new?"

Betty rolled her eyes and whispered to Bilge, "Drop dead, you poot."

Bilge asked, "What did I do?"

"Not you, honey. That poopoo head up there instructing the class."

Longwinded continued, [WHAT ELSE?] "I want you to understand there is a uniform code to bridge openings and that is, none open at the same time. So be sure to read your chart and find out when these bridges open. Don't sound one long blast of the horn and one short because that's what is supposed to be done. Most bridge tenders won't know what you mean and you may drown out part of their favorite TV show. It's best to get on Channel 13 or 16 and beg a little.

"Listen, boots, don't you piss one of these guys off. Bridge tenders have a memory like an elephant and every time your boat approaches his bridge, be ready for punishment.

Another thing that's uniform about bridges is that very few are the same height and the same width, so always consult your charts for height and width.

Longwinded inquired, "Sir, you with the totally disgusted look, where are you going? Why are you leaving the class early?"

The gentleman poised and announced, "After listening to this crap, I'm going to sell my damn boat to my brother-in-law and get even with him."

Longwinded quickly said, "Class, disregard this gentleman's inability to understand the simple rules of the waterway. Now back to whatever subject I was involved in. Oh, I know one thing you can do that helps you to arrive at a bridge at the proper time of opening. Plan the distance between each bridge according to the water currents and the number of kids who might be water skiing. Remember, there will be other boats approaching the bridge the same time as you and there may be some already waiting there. There is a uniform code governing this situation: whoever gets through the sucker first, wins. So always be prepared to get as close as possible to the bridge and when it opens, make a mad dash as soon as you feel you have clearance.

"These rules do not apply to sailboats. Someone in the Bible painted a picture of Jesus on a sailboat and those rag baggers still believe it is His chosen mode of travel, and, they think He's on each one of their damn boats!"

His statement received a lot of "Damn straight, smart ass," accompanied by the bird shot toward the front of the class by the sailboat crowd.

He continued, [WHAT ELSE?] "You powerboaters on your stink pots must realize that sailboaters travel by sail even though most of the time, they're traveling by motor. But they insist on all the benefits and bending of the rules in favor of sailboats. There's a rumor that some damn politician who owned a sailboat created those rules. Well, maybe I better quit while I'm ahead. If I seem to be vacillating back and forth here, my wife just reminded me from the back of the class that we own a sailboat, too, one-eighth, that is.

"One of the major problems overlooked by new skippers

are cross channels. These are channels that cross channels. How does that grab you? So if you're approaching from one direction and you see a strange number appear on the wrong side of the channel and a lot of little day buoys going off by themselves, sailors, you may be in a private channel. Or you may be in another channel going in the opposite direction or a combination of both. Then, of course, there is the channel that divides into two waterways. In the center of this channel is a buoy painted both colors so you can go in either direction. Now how simple can things be?"

Bilge asked, completely befuddled, "Sir, how do I know whether it's a cross channel, a private channel, or something else?"

"This may come as a surprise to you, Mr. Scuppers, but that's what the charts are for even if they really don't make it clear."

Bilge thanked him for his gracious explanation and sat down.

Longwinded continued, "Now, let's get on with it. There is also the preferred side marker which is marked so you can go on either side of it, but one side is preferred over the other for some reason. The government, in their wisdom, and in an attempt to make things simple for everyone, fixed it so there are about a hundred different kinds of markers along the waterway with each meaning something different and some even meaning the same thing."

"Sir, I'm the same Betty Scuppers as before, and what I would like to know is, why don't they make all the markers either red or green and have a different number for each one?"

The instructor's face went pale, fear set into his eyes and his voice became a deathly whisper, "Lady, those are dangerous words. Do you realize what would happen if we made the waterway charts simple to read and the buoys easy to identify? Madness, lady!" He yelled into the mike,"Anarchy! Why, some people think just because the Great Lakes, the inland waterways and the western rivers are within the confines of the United States, that all these waterways should have the same rules. That's a ridiculous idea! Spread by revolutionaries. Don't ever expect the government to do something intelligent like make the rules and buoys the same all over."

Betty meekly asked, "But, sir, if we ask them politely would they change them?"

Longwinded bristled and exploded, "NEVER! If they did that, then all channels would be marked uniform and people could find their way anywhere in our beautiful country. Lady, do you know what that could lead to? People would want to understand their income tax forms, be able to read their insurance policy and expect politicians to tell the truth. Worst of all, they might demand that the government spend our money properly. For Godsakes, woman, that's un-American! That would lead to the end of our right to be confused and bullshitted by our leaders. Why, that might even lead to the TV networks agreeing with the President."

Everyone applauded at his defense of our good ole American way of life. Betty accepted the intelligent rebuke, sat down teary eyed, and whispered to Bilge, "That's so romantic!"

"Anyway, you deep water sailors, let me get off my soap box. There's one other minor detail I'd like to mention and that is sea buoys. No lady, damm it, they don't call them sea buoys because you can see them better. Sea buoys are markers that you follow when coming in from the sea, or going out to the same sea, you see. First thing you have to remember is that their colors are opposite from the ICW buoys, in some places. When you're coming in from the sea, you will see the red buoy on the starboard side and your black or green buoy on the port side. So when you're traveling through the ICW you may cross a sea channel. This will put the opposite color on the opposite side of the ICW. I'm sure you see . . . what I see . . when I tell you how to see this. Except if you're going in the opposite direction then everything you see will be in the opposite direction then everything will be just the opposite, you see."

[THE INSTRUCTOR IS RIGHT AGAIN, YOU SEE.]

The class was nodding their heads.

"Now, class, ranges are the exception. You will find the ranges that are marked on your charts set well back away from the channel so you can line these two aids up and follow them in from the sea and up the channel safely. Now sometimes you will find that one of the lights is used as a beacon. This is usually the lower light or you may call it the forward light. When they use this arrangement you can pass right next to the shorter light in the range. But if the type used is set well back away from the channel, then obviously you'll knock the bottom out of your damn boat if you pass close to it.

"So keep these few pieces of trivia in mind when you're traveling in or near a sea channel. Has everybody got that? I see the little lady in the back taking notes. Read your notes and update the class, please, ma'am."

Betty stood, gave a little curtsy, smiled to the class and said, "If your range is close to the channel, you can go in the opposite direction, though the opposite direction may not be the direction you're going except for when the lights are backways. This allows you to come in from the sea that you're going to or something like that. If you see an eighteen-wheeler coming down the waterway, then get on the grass, I think..."

"Excuse me for interrupting you, Mrs. Scuppers. It's inspirational to see the depth of misconception in this class. Now that we've covered all the simple procedures of chart reading, it would be a good idea for you to spend some time aboard your vessel and contemplate selling the son-of-a-B%$#*&^. If not, then study some of the more complex techniques of safe boating."

Betty confided to Bilge, "You know, honey, I think I've got this whole thing figured out about nautical-legalizing. First, everything comes in multiple choice answers. Then, there's what the sailboat people call it. Then, there's what the sailboat people call us power-boaters. Then, there's what we call them. Then, you have to remember that most of the time if you're going in the opposite direction you have everything on the right side. So, you see how simple it is?"

"I think you're right, Betty. Your notes are going to come in real handy. Betty, I think I kind of dazzled them again with my attire tonight. The little gold anchor on my ascot gave it a simple touch ... understated elegance, that's us, babe. You could tell by the way they were staring at us that they were really dazzled."

Anyway, our two totally confused and mildly convinced heroes left the chart reading class with more than a few questions unanswered.

The instructor ran out into the parking lot in panic and reminded everyone to bring his chart kit the following night. He added, "Remember, sailors, it's really not a kit. It's a book of charts. Though it is a book, it's called a kit."

---

The following night at class everyone joined in the chatter of anticipation. Each little group had studied diligently and was bursting with questions. Weird as it seems at this point, there were intelligent questions about to receive weird answers.

Longwinded proceeded, "Okay class, turn to page thirty-three which says in the right hand corner, 'Page thirty-three joins page thirty-one which joins A which joins twenty-nine which inserts A which is attached to page thirty-five.' Now, they made that quite simple, didn't they?"

Bilge asked, "Sir, what happens to the pages in between?"

"It says, 'Page thirty-two joins page forty-four which represents page four through page nine and page twenty-seven through page thirty-eight.' Now, do you have that clear? As you can see, page thirty-three shows you how to get from Hollywood Beach to Lauderdale-by-the-Sea which is ten miles. But page thirty-two which joins page ten and joins page seventy-five, and, of course, to make the trip in order it joins page forty-four.

"Also, on page thirty-two you will note there is crucial information for the average boater which is how to get permission to do massive ocean dumping in sites 40 CFR parts 220 & 229. Now that should be extremely helpful to us weekend cruisers."

Bilge decided to sit down before he passed out from all that help. The fella seated on the side of Bilge whose mind was blown from the previous night had recuperated enough to get a little more confused. He asked, "Sir, are we going to discuss the color identification of lights and markers on the charts?"

"Why, yes we are. That is a very important question because color identification must be perfectly clear. A good example of this is from North Bay Island to Sunny Island. That's on page thirty-three, class, which joins page twenty-nine. Does everyone have it?

"Sir, you in the back of the class. There is no way you're going to find that on an Exxon road map. They only indicate oil spills, I mean gas stations. You say, you don't have a chart? Then, please join the man on the side of you and look over his shoulder.

"No, lady, it's not in a Florida tour guide map, either.

"Yes, ma'am, the blue stuff is water on a road map, but you can't use it for navigation on the waterway.

"No, ma'am, they don't sell tour guide maps for the waterway.

"Ma'am, you say, you want to know, why not?

"I guess it's just a terrible oversight on the part of the governor. He was under the misconception that if you owned a boat you would buy a chart and that way you would know where you were.

"Now you want to know why the towns are not marked on the buoys like the roads signs on the freeway? Well, ma'am, if you are at the right marker number you should know where you are.

"Yes, you in the middle... not you, ma'am. The one with the red hair who looks like she stuck her finger in a socket. Ask your question. I've already said my prayers."

"Sir, we keep getting lost because the numbers on the markers keep repeating themselves from one place to another. It would help to put the names of the towns on the markers."

"Ma'am, if I were you, I would suggest this to the government because there is a possibility that if it doesn't do any harm, and it doesn't make any sense, and if it costs a lot of money, there is a pretty good chance they'll do it."

The gentleman who was supposed to share with his neighbor, politely covered his chart with his arms and chest, and said, "Buy your own damn chart book." [THIS WAS ANOTHER EXAMPLE OF FRIENDSHIP AND CAMA-

RADERIE THAT EXISTS ON THE WATERWAY.]

"Anyway, class, the little green squares with the odd numbers . . . No, ma'am, they're not oddly written. They're just odd numbers . . . you know, like odd and even.

"Yes, ma'am, one is an odd number, too . . . just not as big as three. Odd numbers are used on black and green day markers.

"Yes, ma'am, you can see them at night when you shine your light on them.

"I know, ma'am, the name is confusing, but we had to call the damn thing something. Please let me continue. The odd numbers marked with little square green ones are on your starboard green side if you happen to be heading north. But, if you're headed south the green markers are on your red side, the port side. Now, on your red side which is your even side or port side and heading north, there is a little red triangle. Now this, of course, is just the opposite if you're headed south.

"Yes ma'am, Mrs. Scuppers, you have a question?"

"On the FL R 4 sec 16 ft. beacon, it shows a little black dot with a little red flag."

"Yes, ma'am, Mrs. Scuppers, that means a flashing red light. It flashes every 4 seconds and is mounted 16 feet high.

"No ma'am, Mrs. Scuppers, the light is not 16 feet high. The structure that the light sits on is 16 feet high. That same little dot with the red flag is on your port side, red."

Betty twisted her head in different directions as she looked at the chart and asked, "Sir, why do they have a little black dot with a red flag on the other side of the channel? It says FL G 4 27, and . . . and the other one on the same side is FL W 6 22. It's also the same color on the charts."

The instructor, having no intelligent reason said, "I don't know, ma'am. It does indicate there's a light there . . . and also indicates the color of the light flashing for night travel."

"Sir, wouldn't it be simpler if they put a little green flag on the green side and the little red flag on the red side and a little white flag where the white light stood?"

"Well, ma'am, with all these government deficits, I imagine they do it to save money."

There was a whole lot of head shaking going on in the

class.

"Let's deal with an insert. On page thirty-three which has the insert on page twenty-nine, we will get a better view of that area. Now, as you can see, at Biscayne Bay there is a broad causeway. This bridge is a bascule bridge with an eighty-foot horizontal clearance. No, lady, it's not eighty feet from the horizon. It's the horizontal clearance of the bridge. Its vertical clearance is sixteen feet.

"Yes, sir, when the bridge is open there is one helluva increase in vertical clearance.

"How many of you know how high your boats are? Hmmmmmm, no one actually knows the height of his boat.

"No, sir, you in the middle of the class, no, sir... It is not necessary to take your boat out of the water and measure it. You measure from the water line to its tallest point for your vertical clearance.

"No, ma'am, if your boat don't fit, it just don't fit... It will be necessary... No, ma'am, if you try it you will either knock the bridge down, tear the hell out of your boat, or kill your damn self. So please measure from the tallest point on your boat to the water line.

"No sir, there's no line on the water. It's on your boat.

"That's right. The blue stripe starts at the red bottom on the side of the white boat. You've got it figured out, sir... No sir, the water line starts at the water no matter where you are on the boat.

"Yes, sir, it is a good idea. God figured that one out.

"You, in the rear of the class. You want to know whether you should measure your boat at high tide or low tide?

"Sir, it doesn't make a damn bit of difference because your boat rises and lowers with the tide.

"Sir, sir! Okay, I give up. If you think your boat will be shorter at low tide and you will fit better through the bridge, then pay your insurance, say goodbye to your friends and ram her through." Longwinded thought, this guy's brain must have stopped last month.

"Ma'am, you say you have a different colored boat. A red bottom with a blue stripe and the rest is white? I think I may have seen one or two others like it along the waterway.

"Well . . . what I'm trying to make clear is the fact that if your boat does not fit under the vertical clearance of a bridge, call on Channel 13 and ask the nice bridge man to open the bridge.

"No, ma'am, he will not open the fixed bridge on the other side.

"Yes sir, you can say that. A fixed bridge is one they fixed so it won't open just to aggravate yachtsmen.

"You said what, sir? Yes, you in the front row looking through the magnifying glasses at the blackboard. You say those are not magnifying glasses, those are your eye glasses. Sir, how old are you? Ninety-five? And you have a boat? Well, sir, tell us all about it. You would rather tell us young ones to go to hell? Why?"

The old man precariously rose to his feet, stared at the class in defiance and said, "Well, if this damn speaker will finally let me say something, I will. I bought a boat because they took my driver's license away, damn functionary, because I'm too old and blind to drive a car. I kept hitting school buses and ambulances and such. Damn things look alike to me, only got into real trouble when I smashed into a cop car, so I bought a fast boat. I don't need no license to go eighty-five miles an hour in my million-dollar cigarette bullet boat. Not only that, I don't have to take one of those damn eye tests, no damn test of any kind. So now I can chase water cops instead of land cops and get in the way just as much. Added to that, there are no damn school buses! Couldn't see one, anyway. Only reason I came here is to see if I could save money on my insurance. I'll be damned if I won't. All I gotta do is sit here and listen to this here bullshit artist and you dummies even if I can't see the blackboard."

[THE OLD MAN IS RIGHT...SICK BUT TRUE.]

"I'm afraid you are right, sir. As long as you use your boat for your own pleasure, no one can stop you from driving it."

"I know that, boy. If anybody is going to get run over by my boat I'm going to do it myself. It's legal up until I kill someone. That's the law or the lack of one. Ain't that nice?"

Bilge whispered to Betty, "That old fart must be a dues paying weirdo."

Longwinded continued, "Sir, you say, you're an insurance man and you're just coming out of shock? At the prices you charge boaters and besides being in shock, you must have a backache from carrying all that money you charge us boaters to the bank."

A round of applause came from the class.

"Yes, ma'am, Mrs. Scuppers, that is Key Biscayne marked on the chart where "Miami Vice" lives. The red line running down the middle of the chart, you'll notice, does not have many buoys, day markers, beacons, towers, ranges, spars, or cans to mark the waterway. It has a course for each direction, 15 degrees if you're going north and the opposite of 180 degrees added if you're going south, 195 degrees . . .

"No, sir, there's no statue at the statute mile marker. It just let's you know when you're at mile 1095.

"No ma'am, it's not marked on the water, either. You think that would be a good idea? Well have at them, babe.

"You have a question? The lady, yes you with the strange far away look. You want to know what day it is? It's Tuesday, lady. You say that's why we are on the wrong page? Now you say page twenty-eight should be on Thursday? That's right, ma'am. That's very awake of you. Now, if you sit there for another two days, you'll be on the right page, that is, if missing persons doesn't find you first.

"Now as you can see, there are various courses heading in various directions. And marked on the chart is the distance between these points. No, ma'am, I don't know why they didn't put mile distances on the long line like they did on the short line.

"Yes sir, if it's 3.7 miles in one direction, it's also 3.7 miles going the other direction.

"You, yes, sir, the one who just woke up. You want to know why Biscayne National Park is a protected area? Sir, that location is set aside to protect it from ourselves. What's that, your children want to know which one of the porpoises is Flipper? Just ask one . . . they're very friendly creatures.

"No, sir, I'm not being a smart ass. I frankly thought the answer to the question was appropriate. You say you're going to quit the class? My horoscope promised me some good news today.

"Okay, let's get into the subject of locks. Although there are none in this particular area, you will encounter them when you cross the Okeechobee Waterway or when you get to the big dark dismal swamp area. Now, how many in this group are familiar with locks? Yes, Mrs. Scuppers, I'm happy to see someone in the class is familiar with locks. Tell us of your experience."

Betty went through a series of eye squints and a curtsy to the class while Bilge beamed with pride. She said, "Lox are little salty fish that a sweet little Jewish lady served us for breakfast. They go best with cream cheese and bagels."

The instructor took several minutes before his bleeding brain could accept her explanation, and he mumbled, "I'm getting to old for this shit. I quit!"

Anyway, with the class ending on that happy note the two winners headed for MY MISTAKE. As they were leaving, Betty became outraged at one of the ladies in the class who asked Bilge what kind of dinghy he had and how big it was. Betty was going to have none of that.

"Bilge, I noticed that naughty grin on your face and you did not rebuke that lady who inquired about your dinghy."

"Betty, I was just being polite like any other man would be whose dinghy was in question. I mean little boat, honey, and my look was one of shock." From the look on Betty's face, he couldn't escape with this bullshit any better than the rest of the male species.

"Betty, what do you think about boaters, poopsy pie?"

"I don't know, Bilge. Maybe you should think."

"Betty, I think they have people just like us out there on that beautiful waterway running around with their boats."

"Bilge, does that sound safe to you?"

"Sure, babe, all the rest of them people are dumb. You remember what that fella said. He thinks there's a law that only crazy people can buy boats or only crazy people buy boats, one or the other. We don't fit into that category, sweetie pie. We're totally different. Remember, Uncle Side Scuppers was nice enough to drop dead so we could get our very own boat. Anyway, poopsy, remember that little rockin' that we was doing the same time the boat was doing a little rockin' . . . pretty good, baby, pretty good."

"I know all this sex talk was brought on by that lady's dinghy question. Disgusting. Men are so disssssssgusting."

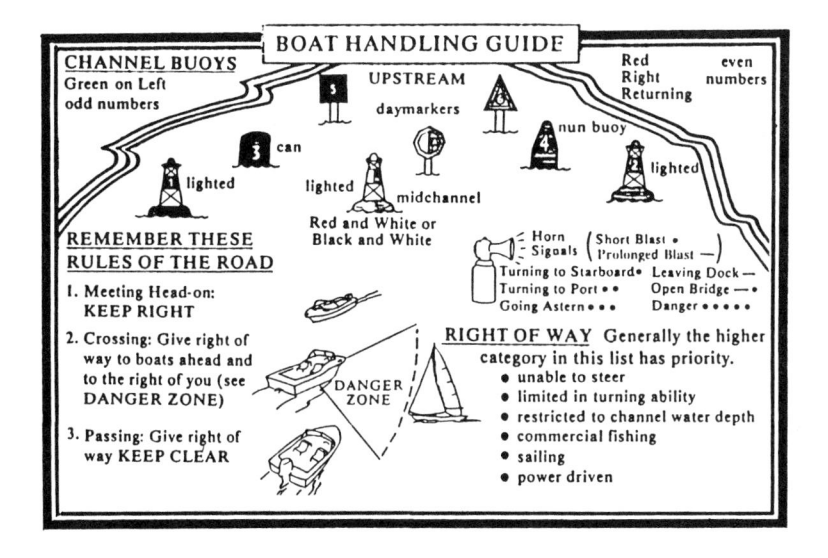

### BOAT HANDLING GUIDE

**CHANNEL BUOYS**
Green on Left odd numbers

UPSTREAM daymarkers

Red Right Returning — even numbers

nun buoy

3 can — lighted
lighted — midchannel
Red and White or Black and White
lighted

**REMEMBER THESE RULES OF THE ROAD**

1. Meeting Head-on: KEEP RIGHT
2. Crossing: Give right of way to boats ahead and to the right of you (see DANGER ZONE)
3. Passing: Give right of way KEEP CLEAR

Horn Signals: Short Blast •  Prolonged Blast —
Turning to Starboard •   Leaving Dock —
Turning to Port • •        Open Bridge — •
Going Astern • • •         Danger • • • • •

**RIGHT OF WAY** Generally the higher category in this list has priority.
- unable to steer
- limited in turning ability
- restricted to channel water depth
- commercial fishing
- sailing
- power driven

## Mid-Channels Markers

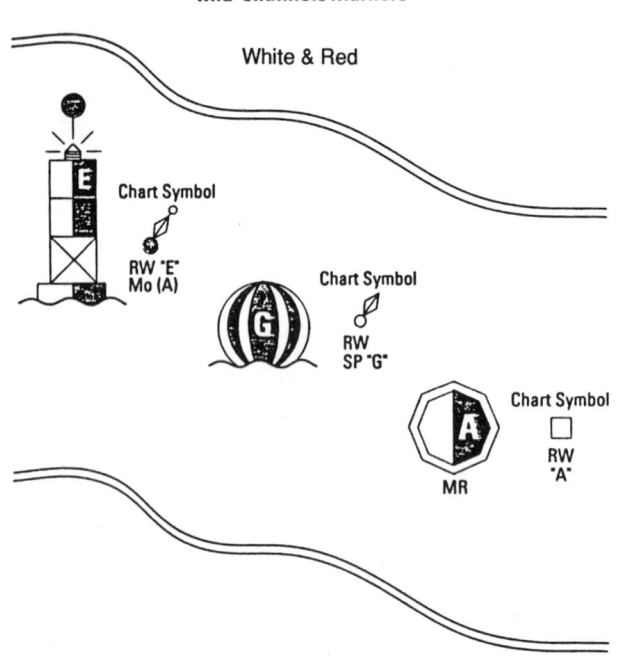

White & Red

Chart Symbol
RW "E"
Mo (A)

Chart Symbol
RW
SP "G"

Chart Symbol
RW
"A"
MR

## Information and Regulatory Markers

Diamond Shape
warns of danger

Diamond Shape
with cross means
boats keep out

Circle marks
area controlled
"as indicated"

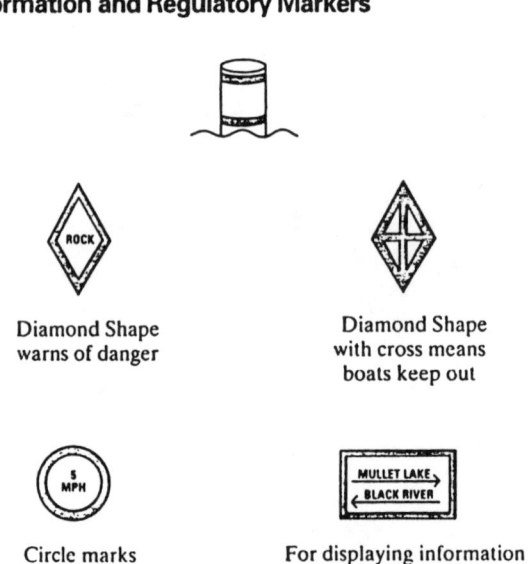

For displaying information
such as directions,
distances, locations, etc.

## Aids to Navigation (cont.)

### Lateral Aids

Lateral aids marking the sides of channels as seen when entering from seaward.

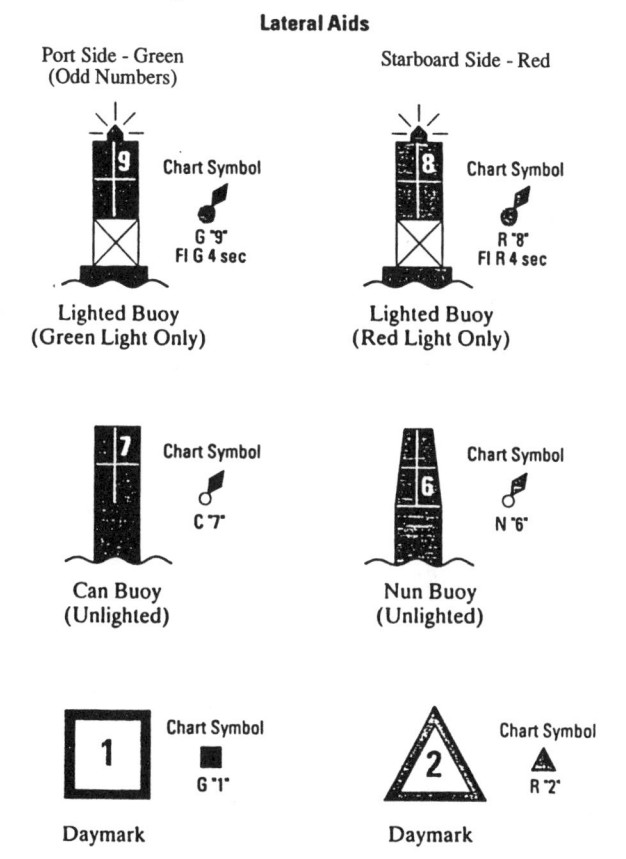

**Lateral Aids**

Port Side - Green
(Odd Numbers)

Chart Symbol
G "9"
Fl G 4 sec

Lighted Buoy
(Green Light Only)

Starboard Side - Red

Chart Symbol
R "8"
Fl R 4 sec

Lighted Buoy
(Red Light Only)

Chart Symbol
C "7"

Can Buoy
(Unlighted)

Chart Symbol
N "6"

Nun Buoy
(Unlighted)

Chart Symbol
G "1"

Daymark

Chart Symbol
R "2"

Daymark

---

Do not tie up to Aids to Navigation, it is dangerous and illegal.

---

55

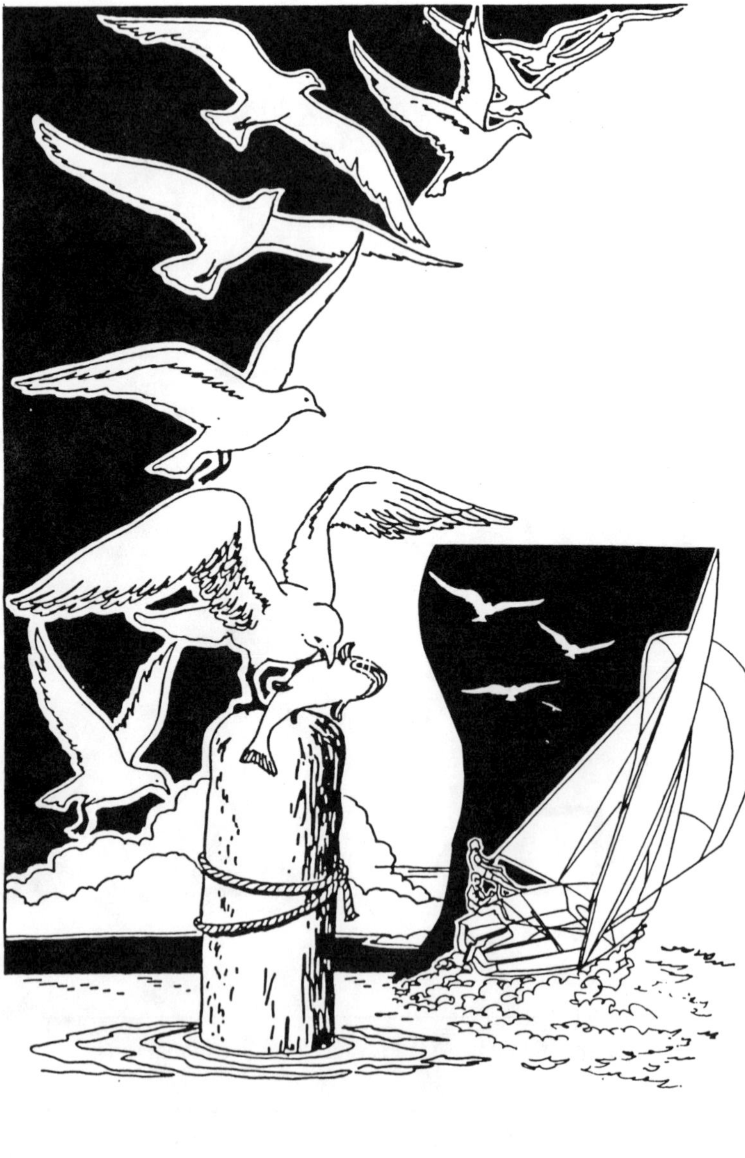

# CHAPTER FIVE

Bilge and Betty developed an immeasurable love for their boat. They declared that owning a boat was the prettiest and bestest thing that ever happened to them. After spending an additional week at the dock of The Sink and Sunk Boatyard and turning on all the equipment at least eighty-three times, Betty fell in love with her two Big Boys and her little girl in the engine room: Big Boy, port engine; Big Boy, starboard engine; and Little Bitty Jenny, generator. It was quite natural that their first spat was over Jenny. Betty kept insisting that Bilge should not turn on too many lights and overwork her.

"Betty, that doesn't have anything to do with it, we're plugged into the dock. Anyway, the generator is small because it doesn't have to do much."

Betty fumed, "That's ridiculous. Just like a man. The Big Boys have nothing to do but move the boat, and us girls have to run everything in the house, and we never get any credit for it. And now you are trying to tell me we are going to get plugged at the dock. That's disgusting. So there."

"Betty, are we having a fuss?" Bilge asked meekly.

Betty stomped her foot, "I'm not fussing. I'm merely saying that you're wrong."

Bilge got in the last word, "Okay, honey."

She loved the sound of her two Big Boys, the way they roared and grumbled and how Bilge made them go VOOM, VOOM. The only problem was the spoiled sport attitude of some of the other boaters, docked at The Sink and Sunk Boatyard. "Imagine all that fuss and confusion," Betty fretted, "just because we started to play with our Big Boys at six o'clock on Sunday morning."

Betty said, "Little girl Jenny has the sweeeeeeetest sound."

Anyway, Bilge didn't believe Jenny was as strong as ole Ragg Bagger said she was. Until he touched the lead wires coming from little Jenny . . . to use ole Bagg of Ragg's expression, "Sure did knocks the hells out of you, didn't it, boy? Shortins' your sex life if you keeps that shits up."

One night just before bedtime Bilge mentioned a terrifying but exciting thought. "Betty, we've been here for three weeks. Why don't we take a trip?"

The idea of cruising should have been mentioned at breakfast, not at bedtime. Consequently, there was damn little sleep that night. The following morning the couple related their plans to Miss Dis-Con-Tent and, needless to say, she was sorry they were leaving. Mr. Snook was elated and presented Betty with a bill for dockage.

Betty squealed with surprise, "You must be kidding, Mr. Smuck!"

"No, I'm not, ma'am."

"Oh yes you are, sir," Betty declared unyielding. "Did we tell you to put our boat there? Did we ask you to tie your electricity to our boat? Did we say anything about being plugged at your dock? And, and is that our water hose or yours?"

Mr. Snook in a steadfast tone replied, "Well, ma'am, it's common knowledge that you have to pay for dockage."

Betty stomped her foot twice in rebuttal, "Sir, we're neither common nor do we use any knowledge. So don't put us in that category. But I will do you the favor of telling everybody you were the one who helped us in our future travels on the waterway."

Mr. Snook tore up the bill and said, "Ma'am, don't do me no favors like that. I don't want the boating world to hold a grudge against me. A crook I am unjustly accused of, a monster I'm not. Goodbye."

---

All the equipment was turned on ... Betty's two Big Boys and Little Jenny. Now, it was time to leave the dock. MY MISTAKE, was tied port side to and a good breeze was coming from that direction supplied by God after the prayers and wishes of everyone at the boatyard.

After the lines were cast off and Bilge got the courage to put the boat in gear, the wind fortunately blew MY MISTAKE away from the dock. Everyone at The Sink and Sunk dock was standing beside his boat with his fenders out in self-defense. A great sigh of relief was heard when the wind forced MY MISTAKE into mid channel.

Betty was a neat little sailor. Although she was left-handed and coiled the lines in the wrong direction, she did twist them into a neat pile. She proceeded to the flying bridge and noticed Bilge admiring the panoramic view as the radar was whirling, the Loran turned on, the radio blaring and every other damn device running that's unnecessary in a well marked waterway. Like many boaters, they believed that there must be a law somewhere saying, "If you've got it on a boat, you damn well better turn it on."

Ole Ragg Bagger watched them from the dock and wondered aloud, "Whys the hell do boaters have their radars operatin' on bright sunny days, runnin' along a well marked channel or in a canal? I guess they's right. Some of them buggers would get lost in their own slip."

Anyway, Betty asked, "Bilge, where are we going?"

............... A long pause .........

"I don't know, Betty. Where do you think we're going?"

She pointed out past the bow, "So far it's that-a-way, Bilge. But I've got a great idea. Remember that lawyer who said we are paid-up members of the Uppity A'ss Marina? I'm sure they'll be very happy to have sailors like us spend some time at our home fort."

"I think it's port, Betty."

"Whichever. Bilge, you're doing so good remembering all those people's advice like keeping the boat reasonably between the red and green posts. Honey, don't you think we should go a little faster than idle?"

"Okay, Betty, I'll goose her up a little."

"Disgusting, men's sex talk."

60

# CHAPTER SIX

MY MISTAKE, a vessel capable of cruising at fifteen knots, was speeding along the waterway at a dazzling speed of five knots and occupying both sides as well as the middle of the channel. Bilge steered a course that would break a snake's back.

Betty panicked, "Oh, my God, Bilge, what's that thing up ahead? It looks like a fence all across the water."

"I think it's a bridge, Betty. What do your notes say to do?"

"It says we're supposed to call Mr. Thirteen on the channel."

"Give him a call, Betty. Ole Bagg of Raggs taught us how to use the radio. Go ahead, honey."

Before Betty was in the process of switching over to Channel 13 from Channel 16, she overheard the Coast Guard trying to get the location of a vessel that was in distress. Three boaters were interrupting the distress call on Channel 16 with trivial conversation. The Coast Guard begged the other boaters to clear the airways so they could attempt to rescue one of their fellow boaters. Their pleas fell on deaf ears and loud mouths.

Anyway, Betty switched over to Channel 13, pressed the button, and using her best nautical-legalizing tone, she called, "Mr. Thirteen on bridge channel? Mr. Bridge Channel, do you mind getting out of the way so we can pass? My husband doesn't like to wait because we're from New York."

"Lady, if you're for real, this is the bridge tender. The bridge does not open for another twenty-five minutes due to heavy auto traffic this time of day. Please have your vessel stand by."

"Sir, our boat is not standing. It's floating here by your bridge."

The bridge tender looked out of the window and saw Bilge turn the boat in nine directions in an attempt to hold the vessel in mid-channel. "This is the bridge tender. Ma'am, what is that bright shining object on your flying bridge?"

"Oh, Mr. Bridge Channel, that's my husband in his new captain's hat and blazer. And we really would appreciate it if you would get your bridge out of our way."

The bridge tender was thinking, there's a law against this shit, but I'm going to open the bridge and let these two go before I start believing the soap stories on TV are true.

The bridge tender tied up rush hour traffic for miles as Bilge took twenty minutes to work his panicky way through the bridge. Betty kept running up and down the sides of the boat diligently looking for the toll basket to throw her quarters in.

When she returned to the flying bridge, Bilge stood frozen into place, hands shaking and white as a ghost. "Betty," he said gasping for breath, "we came through a little bit sideways, but we made it."

"Oh, Bilge, you're such a great captain. Honey, do you think we'll get into trouble? I couldn't find the toll basket to throw my quarters into. Did you see all those nice drivers on the bridge waving at us? I wonder what those sweet people were saying? They all seemed to be giving us the power-to-the-people sign with one finger pointed straight up . . . or something like that! But Bilge, you were right. I couldn't find any toll baskets, so everything on the waterway must be free."

"I told you, Betty, I told you that it's not going to cost us anything to own a boat."

As they proceeded on their wobbly way down the waterway, Betty said, "Oh God, Bilge, look at that island coming towards us!"

"Betty, you're going to have to start wearing your glasses. That's one of those knights of the waterway pushing a whole bunch of barges. Give him a call, darlin'. You do it so good."

Betty switched over to Channel 16 and heard the last of the May Day call from the boater in distress saying, "Don't bother you bunch of son-of-a B#$%%$##$*. The boat has already sunk!"

"Yooo hooo, Mr. Barge Boat man, this is us! And we can see you right in front of us. Which side do you want us to pass on? The port side, the starboard side, or the middle?"

"This is 2138, the M.V. Reb Hustler. Ma'am, I think ya'll

already have both sides and the middle. So here's a little advice; why don't you just get the hell out of the channel and let me go by since there's plenty of water on both sides."

"Yooo hooo sir, no sir. We only need plenty when it's deep and we don't intend to anchor. So I'd advise you, sir, that we were here first. But we will let you decide where you want to pass."

The Reb Hustler, only weighing two thousand times more than MY MISTAKE, was forced to be a true knight of the waterway. Because, he was pushing 18,000 barrels of hi-test gasoline, and was convinced these two idiots heading toward him would turn the waterway into a bonfire. Terror often forces politeness, so he got the hell out of the way and allowed the two heroes to pass. They were waving madly as they went by with Betty blowing kisses.

Heading north and passing through Port Everglades, they came upon a section of a channel that had several interesting markings, especially to a new sailor. Their radar showed a whole bunch of good things. If they had followed the green channel off to the starboard which was proper, they would have emerged safely. But anyone looking at the chart of this area could see why our two sailors became hopelessly lost. They went straight instead. The marker, helping in the confusion, was a triangle, a number two, which is proper but the wrong color. And on the same side of the channel is a square green marker, marker number three, which is also proper. This is no problem for experienced sailors.

Near hysteria, Betty asked, "Bilge, where do you think we are?"

"Well, Betty, we are one of a few places. We're either headed for Tarpon Bend or we're heading into these people's backyard called Rio Vista Isles or we're going east which will eventually be north."

"Bilge, why don't we look at the radar?"

"I'm looking at it, Betty, but it's got a zillion things on it."

"What are those little dots?"

"Those are the beacons and day markers, Betty."

"But it doesn't show any numbers or colors. How do they expect us to know which one is which?"

"You're supposed to look at the numbers on the beacons, Betty."

"I can see that, silly goose, but how do I match them up with the ones on the radar? The radar doesn't show any numbers."

"Look, Betty. We're either here at the green one pointing east on the west side near to number three or we're by this other number one green close to the other number three green going the other way."

"Bilge, now that we have that worked out, I still don't see any numbers on the radar set."

"Betty, I don't know if it's supposed to have numbers on it, but it would make sense if it did. Maybe something's wrong with the set."

Bilge continued on his way and finally blundered into the main channel which headed north past Bahia Mar Yacht Club. Bilge was occupied with the terror of approaching another bridge. Betty fumed over the radar set for not showing any numbers. She stomped her foot while squinting her eyes at the radar set.

She said, "Bilge, give me the instruction book on that radar set. I'm going to find out who the manufacturer is and complain. I know how to complain because I was the head of the complaint department. And, as you know us New Yorkers are experienced complainers!"

Betty opened the manual as Bilge was approaching a bridge that he thought he could pass under. Terrified as he proceeded under the bridge, Bilge clutched the wheel with both hands and at this moment in destiny Betty spotted the name of the manufacturer.

"Yeeeeooooowwwww! Bilge, look at this!"

Bilge, thought the bridge was falling on him, and had the feeling that at any moment he was going to have to change his diaper. Slamming the vessel in reverse, he damn near ran over two smart asses jumping his wake with water scooters. [WHICH WAS NOT A BAD IDEA!] Then he slammed the vessel full ahead again and dashed under the bridge scattering the oncoming water traffic. He finally got control of himself and the vessel and began to breathe again. With panting breaths, he said,"Betty, if you ever do that again... so help me, I'm going to give you my meanest frown. Betty, why did you frighten me? I thought you said that this bridge is one of the ones that we can pass under safely."

"Sorry, Bilge, honey, I was a little confused. I haven't worked out whether it's a fixed vertical or a fixed horizontal or which one is high or which one is wide, but that's not important. We made it. Quit shaking, Bilge, and look at who the manufacturer of this radar set is. It's I. Happily Fung U.S. Electronics... of all things a Japanese company. Bilge, I'm writing a letter of complaint about my complaint right now."

"Do it, Betty. It'll give me time to recover from my heart attack."

> Dear Mr. I. Happily Fung U.S. and everyone else in your company:
> I wish to complain because I know how to complain and you will realize that when I complain that I am a competent complainer. After all that we have done for your country and forgiving you for making your cars too small for Americans, my husband says that he is sure your radar set, your number one Fung Up Special, is either faulty or behind the times.
> He is sure and he assures me that he is sure that the Americans are surely coming out with a radar set that's sure to show the numbers are on the beacons on the waterway.
> So, are you sure that your set should not show the numbers? Or, are you surely behind the times... of that I am sure.
> Yours surely,
> Betty Scuppers

Anyway, when this devastating letter reached the president of the Japanese manufacturer, I. Happily Fung U.S. Electronics, headquartered in downtown Los Angeles, it created ripples of fear throughout the entire corporation.

The president immediately called a staff meeting and informed his herd of listeners that he had received from an absolutely reliable source that the Americans are coming out with a radar set that shows the numbers on the beacons along the waterway. Panic raced through the listeners.

The Japanese, true to their gentlemanly technique of doing business in their polite and dignified way, immediately imported two thousand forty-year-old students and entered them as freshman at California universities with the sole purpose of politely stealing the whole damn idea.

---

After travelling thirty-five miles and experiencing an exhilarating, partly terrifying, and mostly confusing journey, MY MISTAKE entered the south end of Lake Worth as darkness was approaching.

"Bilge, are we going to have to anchor?"

"Yeah, Betty. I've got the whole thing worked out. Here's the button that says, 'anchor up and anchor down.' My problem is, are we going to anchor up or are we going to anchor down? If we're going to anchor up, the anchor is up and we have to go down. But if we're going to anchor down, then the anchor has to go down so we can anchor up. Remember, ole Ragg Bagg said when you get to the right spot just anchor up."

"I don't know, Bilge. They say here on the instructions that we're supposed to just anchor."

"Here's the way I figure it, Betty. First we've got to select a safe spot where the water is deep and we know right where we are. Now according to this map, chart, I'm sorry, Betty, chart . . . the deepest water is right between the red and green markers. So I think this would be the best spot."

"You're definitely right, Bilge, because this is where all the boats and ships pass and we definitely know where we are. I think. So, honey, I'm going to go down there and watch the anchor fall overboard. You stop the boat."

"Betty, I think the anchor is supposed to do that."

Bilge reached over and with a shaking finger hit the anchor down button. It went overboard with a rush and plunged into the water. Unfortunately, Bilge was still moving at idle. The anchor hooked into the bottom and laid out about 200 feet of line before Bilge had the courage to take his finger off the button. The anchor dug into the bottom of the channel as MY MISTAKE was snatched around in a circle.

Bilge panicked and hit the kill button on both engines. MY MISTAKE, was jerked to a stop by her anchor line and swung gently back and forth in mid ship channel. Bilge peeked over the top of the windshield. All looked safe. He then stood proudly and announced, "We did it, Betty, and there was nothing to it!"

"Bilge, darling, don't you think we have too much string let out on the boat? It might cause us to get out of the channel."

"No problem, Betty. I'm an expert at this now."

Bilge was confident due to the fact that there was only one other direction for that button to go. He pressed anchor up and retrieved enough anchor line to allow MY MISTAKE to swing back and forth safely in the middle of the ship channel.

Of course, no one informed Bilge about anchor lights or the danger of anchoring in the middle of a ship channel when they had attended Power Squadron classes. But this minor detail, the possibility of getting run over by a ship, was lightly considered as the class muddled through the rest of the confusing instructions.

Our two heroes missed the pleas of the Coast Guard requesting that all safety features should be required learning and that a license should be obtained to operate a vessel.

The Scuppers were told by their insurance company that if you get a license or attend classes you do receive a discount on your insurance. This way, if someone is using the same insurance company as you and doesn't have a license and runs over your butt, the insurance company saves money. I think!

The Coast Guard will remind you, if asked, that they do not have the power to require anyone to learn the rules of the waterway, they can only hope.

Anyway, one of the most romantic and not always comfortable events a person can experience aboard a vessel is to anchor out. When all conditions are good, which happens occasionally, this is a peaceful and beautiful time in boating. The gentle swing of the boat, the soft sounds of the night, the twinkling of lights along the shore allow moments of unsurpassed tranquility. Especially after a good sundowner drinkie poo on the bow. This is the time when a man can get in touch with nature. It's tranquilizing and it's beautiful. 'IF' there are no bugs, no thunderstorms, and a lack of jerks running around making wakes of six foot seas. The night calls of birds, the splashing of fish in a mad dash for safety . . . Ahhhhhhh . . . it can be very memorable.

Betty and Bilge spent their first exciting night at anchor. As most boaters have experienced, but few admit, they jumped up at every creak and rock of the boat and checked their position a dozen times.

Betty, like most wives, drove Bilge crazy by repeatedly telling him that the anchor was dragging. She screamed each time another vessel approached. "They're going to hit us. I just know it . . . Well, no, they didn't. This time."

Bilge reminded Betty that they were in no danger because they were anchored safely in the middle of the ship channel. But God is kind. The darlings settled down for the night and turned off MY MISTAKE's ship-to-shore radio and listened to the tranquil music of Little Richard and Elvis Presley. Consequently, they were spared all the sweet comments of their fellow mariners when they were forced to slow down to go around MY MISTAKE anchored in the middle of the channel.

"Bilge, aren't those people darling! Each and everyone of them who passed us, slowed down and yelled greetings. I wish I could hear what they said."

The next morning Bilge got a bright idea. "Betty, you know, I think we should try out our dinghy before we pull up anchor. I don't think we could find a better place."

"Bilge, you've been talking too sexy since we've been on this boat. Anyway, someone might see us when they drive by."

"Not my dinghy, Betty. The one on the back of the boat."

"Oh, that one, Bilge. We have to come to an understanding about that little boat's name. I will not stand for that vulgar name being used on our cute little boat. Remember, we agreed that 'dinghy' was a very bad word, even for yours, so we called it your 'doololley'. And even when it thinks it's a big man, we call it our little soldier standing up straight trying to get attention from Mommy. So I want to call it the Little Baby Boat Carried By The Daddy Boat."

"Okay, Betty, but I'm going to try it out. Let's see now, if we loosen this line . . . Hold this one, Betty, and I'll loosen this line . . . ."

Betty only heard "loosen this line" and the bow of the dinghy hit the water with a bang scaring the hell out of Bilge. He turned his end loose and the dinghy was launched with a double splash.

He said, "Betty, it was a little splashy but it worked out real good," as he made a wobbly and holding-on-to-everything boarding of the dinghy.

Betty called down, "Bilge, do you know how to start it?"

Bilge shouted back, "Piece of cake, Betty. Remember that dummy in garden appliances who got his finger cut off showing some jerk how sharp the blades were on that lawnmower and the guy's kid hit the starter button? Wango . . . one missing finger. Remember, honey, I was the one they said would be the best choice to take that dummy's place for two weeks. Babe, these outboard motors are nothing but lawnmowers on water, a piece of cake."

There is one minor thing Bilge forgot. One is on land and must be pushed to make it move; the other is on the water. When Bilge pulled the starter cord, the damn thing just took off like a bat out of hell with Bilge holding on for dear life and not to the steering handle. But God is kind to drunks and fools.

Anyway, the Little Baby Boat Carried On The Back Of The Daddy Boat came to a stop about a hundred yards away with Bilge standing up, waving, and calling to Betty for help.

On a scale of 1 to 10, receiving help from Betty was a minus four. He had a better chance of the Ayatollah becoming Jewish. Ah, but Betty's quick mind went into action

"My, my, my, I wish Bilge would stop all that yelling and waving. Anyone can see he's in trouble. Let's see now, the Coast Guard man said when it's a case of life and death you were to call Channel 16 and say it was some kind of day."

Betty watched Bilge float away waving and screaming his head off. She thought, look at him making a spectacle of himself. He's acting just like a husband and yelling that if I don't do something right away he is going to kill me. Poot on him...

"Now what did he say about the radio? Hmmmmmm... turn it on, press the button, and say what kind of day it is... Yooooo hoooooo, Mr. Coast Guard man... July seventh day... July seventh day..."

The petty officer of the watch at the Coast Guard Station, standing by on the radio was staring at the receiver wondering if somebody at the local nuthouse broke loose and got hold of a radio.

Betty had her hands full waving at Bilge and repeating over and over, "July day... July day... July day..."

The petty officer of the watch said, "Lady, this is the United States Coast Guard to the vessel calling. You are not supposed to use this station except for an emergency. This is a standby station only."

"OOOOOOhhh, that's wonderful. I'm glad I got the right Coast Guard. I didn't want one of those foreign types who wouldn't understand what I was saying."

"I'm sorry, lady, but I don't know what you're saying, either."

"Well, if you listen closely you will hear me say, 'July Day, July Day, July Day' and I think it's the seventh. By the way, young man, what's your name?"

"Petty Officer Foul-Up, ma'am. And I heard you loud and clear but I don't understand what you mean. Are you trying to say May Day?"

"Definitely not, young man. This is the month of July and it wouldn't make any sense to say May Day in the wrong month. Now would it? We're in enough trouble as it is without reporting the trouble we're in in the wrong month."

Petty Officer Foul-Up decided to go along with this nut to find out if there was a real problem. He recalled the last problem he had handled which ended in, "Don't bother, you son-of-a-%@#$%%*. The boat just sank."

He said, "I think you are right, lady. That dumb May Day never made any sense to me, anyway."

Guess who just walked in? That's right . . . Commander May Day. He said, "I'm glad to hear that, Petty Officer Foul-Up. Your next assignment is at Ice Station Zero at the North Pole. It'll give you time to think about whether I make sense or not."

"I didn't mean you, sir. There is a lady calling in a July day instead of a May Day for what I think is a bit of trouble. So, I'm going along with her to find out what's going on."

"Lady, what is the name of your vessel?"

"MY MISTAKE."

"Lady, are you saying your call is a mistake? If it is a mistake, please clear the airways."

"No, Mr. Petty Foul, my call is not a mistake. She, its name, now listen closely so you don't foul up . . . MY MISTAKE."

Commander May Day recognized the caller and the danger to the future of the service and decided to take command instead of using good judgment and sneaking out the door. While trying to control the fear in his voice, he said, "You better let me handle this, F-Up I mean, Foul-Up."

With a trembling hand he pressed the button and said, "Hello, Mrs. Scuppers. This is Commander May Day. Do you have a problem?"

"Yes sir, I do and one of my problems is with your hired help. I know how hard it is to get good help nowadays but on government pay it would seem like you could get the best."

Meanwhile, out on the waterway, Bilge was drifting out of sight.

Betty continued, "I can also see why you call him a petty type of officer. That is exactly the way he is handling this whole thing."

"Besides that, Mrs. Scuppers, what can we do to help you and get the airways cleared? Do you have a case of life and death?"

"Oh that, I almost forgot. Bilge is in the Little Baby Boat we carry on the back of the Daddy Boat and he's drifting away."

"Mrs. Scuppers, exactly where are you located at this time?"

"I'm on the boat."

"That's fine, ma'am, but what I would like to know is, what is your position?"

"On what subject?"

The commander's fingernails were chewed to the quick by now. He said, "By position, I mean the boat."

"I'm on the highest deck leaning against the dashboard, talking on the radio, and trying to see my husband through the spy classes. I can only look out of one side of the spy glasses because when I look out of two sides of the spy glasses, I see two of everything and I only need to see one of everything."

Commander May Day screamed into the mike, "Mrs. Scuppers, WHERE is the boat located?" He lowered his voice and pleaded, "Where is the boat located at this time? Please think before you answer."

"Oh, that's easy. It's in the water."

The commander started to bite the mike, but control is everything when in command. "Ma'am, in the water, where? Do you see anything to help us locate your position so we can determine where you are if you need assistance?"

"Oh, I don't need any assistance."

"Then, Mrs. Scuppers, what is this all about pleeeeease?"

"Don't get upset, Commander Doodleday. It's my husband who is floating away and needs assistance. What's wrong with you people? If we didn't need help why would we call?"

"Ma'am, look out the window and tell me what kind of markers you see."

"Well, there's a big green one and a big red one and the boat's in the middle. Also my husband said the island over on the right is where you grow peanuts."

"That's just fine, Mrs. Scuppers. You are in the right place for now. Just stay there. That's the ship channel."

"Oh, sir, I can't go anywhere anyway. We are anchored real good."

"Holy shit! I mean, Ma'am, you can't anchor there. That's a ship channel. Please move right away."

"What is the matter with you, sir? We know it's a ship channel. There's a rude ship getting in my husband's way right now. Anyway, didn't you say I was in the right place? Besides, there are some good reasons why I will not move. First, I don't know how to get the fish hook out of the water. Second, I don't know how to turn the boat on. Third and the most important, my husband would be mad at me when he came back and found me gone. So there, smarty pants."

The commander quickly gave orders to send a cutter out to get those screwballs out of the ship channel before someone ran over their dumb ass and made his day.

"Mrs. Scuppers, we have help on the way. Can you see your husband through the spy glasses and if you can, please tell me what he is doing?"

"Yes, I can still see him. He is trying to tell a group of squinty-eyed people running around a very big ship that his motor won't start. They are doing a lot of waving and he is pointing to the motor and shaking his head. He is also, oh, my goodness that's a very naughty thing for him to say to those people on the ship with his finger."

The commander sat down and started to do the only thing he thought would do any good. He started to pray.

Our hero, Bilge, was pointing to his motor, shaking his head and yelling at the top of his voice to the people on the ship. "The goddamn thing won't start. You made the damn thing, if you want to help me, come down here and start the freaking piece of junk. And no, you dumb shits, no matter how much you wave your hands back and forth, I'm not Mary Poppins and I damn well can't fly." Bilge was becoming infuriated. He shot the bird to the captain and yelled, "Consider this a protest from all of US to all of you."

The seven-hundred foot Japanese freighter was backing down at flank speed. Bilge drifted alongside when she stopped her engines. His rubber dingy bumped gently along her sides as he passed under her stern. Bilge looked up to get the ship's name so he could complain to his congressman. It read, RIP OFF MARU.

Finally, the Coast Guard cutter, Brave Soul named for putting up with recreational boaters, arrived. One of the seamen, Petty Officer Do-Nothing, asked, "Sir, should we take the gentleman aboard or just take him in tow?"

Lieutenant Blowhard sputtered, "Just take him in tow because if he comes aboard, I will personally kill that crazy son-of-a-b%@#$$*."

"Lieutenant Blowhard, don't you think it would be better if you came out of the rope locker and instructed these people on the right way to anchor? Sir, I think we should at least give them a citation."

"Petty Officer Do-Nothing, just call Commander May Day for further instructions and leave me the hell alone."

"Commander May Day, this is Petty Officer Do-Nothing. Sir, we have just delivered Mr. Scuppers to his boat. Lieutenant Blowhard instructed me to call you for further instructions."

"Do-Nothing, where in the hell is the lieutenant?"

"He is hiding in the rope locker, sir."

"Good man, good man, for a moment I feared he was trying to talk sense to that idiot Scuppers. Tell him to remain there until he feels safe. Those idiots, idiotics are contagious. My instructions, are a direct order! Get the fuc*& away from those two while it is still safe. I don't want to lose any more good men."

As the cutter cast off, Do-Nothing said, "Goodbye, Mr. Scuppers. By the way, did you turn the gas on on your outboard motor?"

With a sheepish look, Bilge asked, "Turn what gas on?"

"That's what I thought, sir. Goodbye, Mr. Scuppers."

Do-Nothing radioed Commander May Day and reported, "Sir, we are leaving the Scuppers now. However, the Japanese want to make a protest."

"Good, tell them to take it up with General Conglomerate Motors."

Anyway, after lots of hugs and kisses and two fusses getting the dinghy aboard, our two sailors were together again and ready to start their trip north.

Betty's mood changed. Suddenly came the foulest most disgusting words a wife can say to her husband. Bilge got it double-barrelled. "Don't you think it would be a good idea to read the instructions, Bilge?"

He bravely answered, "Betty, reading instructions is for dummies."

That morning the Coast Guard stopped all vessels that approached the hazardous position of MY MISTAKE now in the process of readying to lift her anchor. The line of halted vessels included one eastbound tanker trying to leave port, several yachts and one pissed-off Japanese captain of an automobile delivery ship writing a Mo-tuff shitty-Mo letter to General Conglomerate Motors.

Bilge placed his shaky fingers on the button to retrieve their anchor. Betty ran back and forth to the galley getting pails of water to wash the mud off her pretty anchor. They headed north full of inspiration and excitement towards their home port, Uppity A'ss Marina, at Lake Worth.

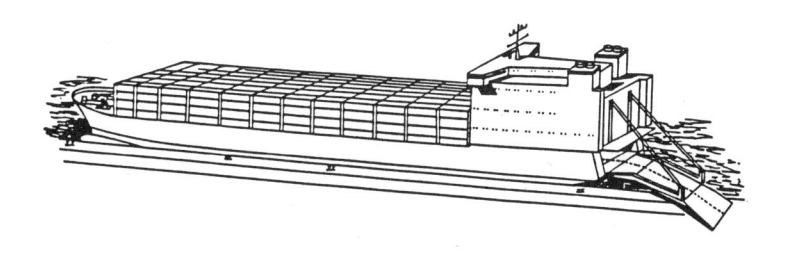

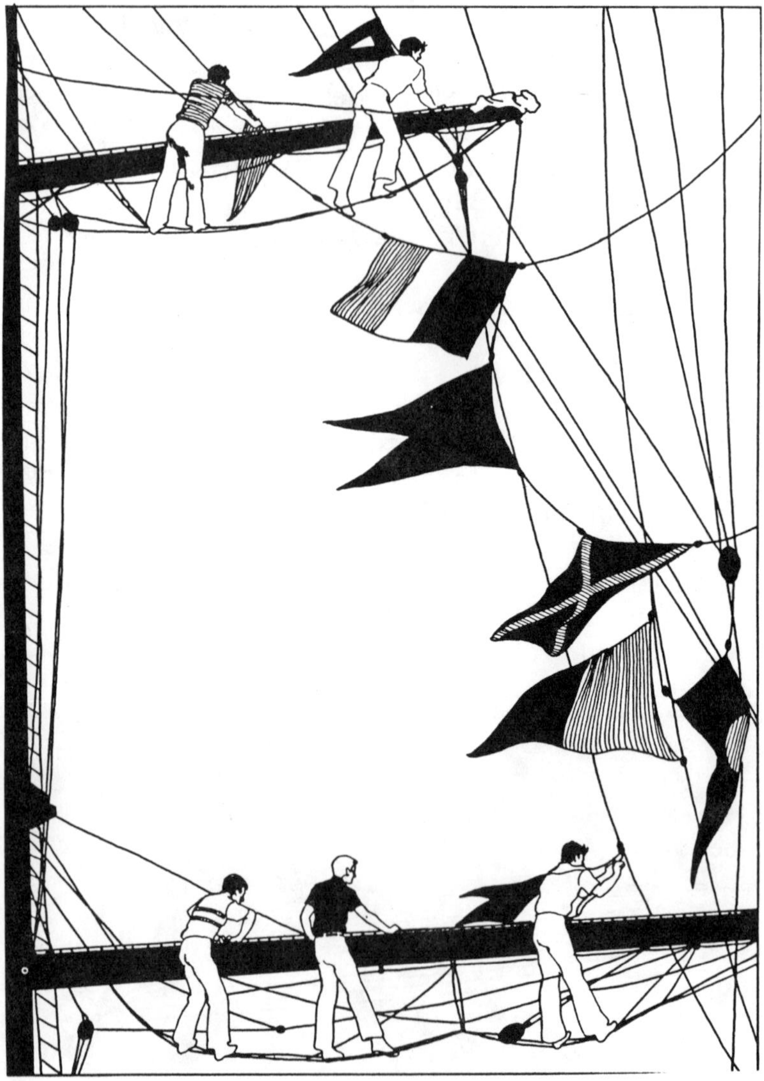

# CHAPTER SEVEN

The north end of Lake Worth is a very interesting place to approach, especially for two inexperienced sailors.

"Okay, Betty, my little pretty chart reader, where do we go from here?"

"Weeellllll, let me see. We left Lake Worth inlet and we got around that island where the Coast Guard grows peanuts ... now we go straight. Bilge, don't you think those people who work for the government get upset over the minutest problems?"

"Betty, it's crazy. They've got some of the best paying jobs and did you ever hear of anyone getting fired by the government? Just think, they have nothing better to do than ride around on boats taking care of us. Now, how easy can you have it? You know, Betty, I wonder how Commander May Day and his employees would have handled one of my problems at the department store, like trying to convince a fat woman she's buying undersized drawers?"

"You're right, Bilge. We made a minor complaint about you going adrift which was a very serious situation. It should have been handled in a minor manner. But if you don't go straight, Bilge, we're going to run into that island."

"Oh, that island. Piece of cake, sweet patooty. Try the radio for a checker. You know, we always have to be on our toes."

By now, Betty was an old hand at using the radio. Using her best nautical slang, she pressed the button and said, "Yooooooo hooooo, everybody out there. Good morning! Is yours working? Please say something so I can see if mine is working, too. Over the wilco and riggers the out, or is it Mr. Rogers or something like that?"

One smart ass, half-stoned from the previous night, picked up his speaker and said, "Mine worked last night, lady, but I don't know whether it will work this morning. Would you like to try it?"

Betty answered, "I'm sure it's okay, mister. Whatever

you're doing with your hand is making it work real good. Just keep pushing your button and talking into the end of it and it will go off real loud."

"Smart ass broad."

"Bilge, I wonder what was wrong with him. Did I say something wrong?"

"Ooooooooooh, no, Betty, darling, you did just fine. I couldn't have said it better myself."

Gripping the wheel and waving at everybody who was brave enough to pass them, Bilge said, "Betty, what the hell's going on up there with those markers? Check the chart quickly. Check the waterway guide, too."

Betty was waving and calling to the porpoises by the bow. "Hello, Flipper. Hello, Flipper and your friends. Bilge, look at the baby Flipper."

"Betty, check the chart or we'll be swimming with Flipper."

"Weeeeellllll, the guide doesn't say anything and . . . Oh, my, my, my, Bilge. Look at all those markers. Let's see, there are some green ones on the red side and some red ones on the . . . Oh, poo, Bilge. Why don't we just go in between all of them and that way we can't miss."

"Atta, girl, pilot, your idea is working."

MY MISTAKE bumped gently across the sand bar at high tide and into the channel leading to the north end of Lake Worth.

[GOD WAS TAKING CARE OF HIS INNOCENT FOOLS, THAT'S WHY I FEEL SAFE WRITING THIS NUTTY BOOK.]

"We're in the channel now, Betty. Call Uppity A'ss Marina and let them know we're coming."

"It's Uppity A'ss Marina, Bilge. Hello, hello, hello. Yoooo hoooo! Is anybody at Uppity A'ss home? We're right here and we are coming home to visit you."

"This is Ding-a-Ling at Uppity AAAAAAA'ss Marina to the vessel calling. Switch over to sixty-nine on your vessel, please."

"What does she mean by that, honey, and why do you have that naughty look on your face?"

Looking like a bird that swallowed two cats, Bilge said, "Oh, I'm sure she means another channel."

Betty switched over and heard, "This is Uppity AAAAAA'ss Marina, back to the vessel calling."

"Bilge, do you think they mean us? After all, we are the vessel that is doing the calling to the person that is doing the calling, aren't we?"

"Betty, we are the vessel calling the one who is answering our call, I think."

"This is MY MISTAKE, calling you, I think."

"What mistake?"

"Calling you, Uppity A'ss Marina."

"Thank you for calling. This is Uppity AAAAAAAA'ss Marina, clear. Switching over to Channel 16."

"Bilge, that rude person doesn't want to talk to us."

"There must be some mistake, Betty. I'll handle this."

"This is MY MISTAKE calling Uppity A'ss Marina. Come aboard."

"This is Uppity AAAAAAAA's Marina. You already said it was your mistake, skipper. Uppity A'ss, clear."

"It is MY MISTAKE, not was my mistake, lady."

"Thanks for the English lesson, mister, but a mistake is a mistake so why don't we just forget the whole thing."

"Lady, this is MY MISTAKE, and I don't want to forget MY MISTAKE."

"Well, sir, if you want to suffer over this, go right ahead."

"Ma'am, if you don't want to talk about MY MISTAKE, when I get there you will see MY MISTAKE for yourself. By the way, I don't see how my Uncle Side Scuppers could have kept his boat there."

"Oh, that MY MISTAKE . . . Oh yes, I know MY MISTAKE. Now . . . sheeee-it's your MISTAKE which is my mistake for not recognizing that you were trying to tell me that your mistake was MY MISTAKE. That's wonderful. You're the Scuppers with all the pees. Now that we have all that straightened out, come and tie right up. Come in the office afterward and we will get you fixed right up. Now, how is that?"

[If YOU WERE ON THE FLYING BRIDGE WITH THE

TWO SWEETHEARTS, YOU WOULD SMELL THE RUBBER BURNING FROM A FEW OF THE WIRES IN THEIR HEADS TRYING TO SORT THAT ONE OUT.]

"Betty, we better ask about an oil change. Miss Fuller Something said the boatyard did everything but that."

"Hello, hello, yoooo hooo, Ding-a-Ling. This is Betty, afloat on MY MISTAKE. Do you give oil changes?"

"Hi, Mrs. Scuppers. This is Ding-a-Ling. Yes, we do. It's one of the services we provide. I'll let you speak to the man who makes the arrangements."

"Uppity A'ss Marina back to MY MISTAKE. This is Mr. Daily Sufferer, the manager. What can we do for you, lady?"

"Hello, Mr. Suffering Manager, this is mated Betty. Do you give oil changes?"

"Uppity A'ss back. What kind of boat do you have and what kind of engines, ma'am? If you supply me with that information, we will have everything ready when you arrive to give you a quick oil change."

"Yooo hoooo, this is me again. The boat is a big white one with a blue stripe and the two Big Boy engines are gray. They make lots of noise and make the boat go. Also, there is a little green engine that doesn't make the boat go, but it makes the lights work."

Ding-a-Ling asked, "Okay, boss. How are you going to handle this one?"

"You know, Ding-a-Ling . . . I think anything I ask her now is going to screw this intelligent conversation up even more."

The boss took the smart man's way out by saying nothing. Ding-a-Ling thought, men are cowards.

"Uppity AAAAAAAAA'ss Marina calling MY MISTAKE. By the way, Mrs. Scuppers, I forgot to ask you. Do you have any pets on board?"

"Only my husband, Ding-a-Ling, and I can assure you he's housebroken."

Mr. Sufferer turned to Ding-a-Ling and asked, "Okay, Miss Wise'n Ass. How are you going to handle that one?"

Ding-a-Ling remained silent. The boss thought, women are chicken sheets.

Meanwhile, our two boatmen were making their approach

to the harbor.

"This is Gay-One, the dockmaster at Uppity A'ss Marina on Channel 69. Mr. Scuppers, is that your boat coming into the harbor sideways?"

With Bilge handling the starboard engine and Betty handling the port engine, they both had their hands full. But Bilge managed to grab the radio speaker, "I'm not sure, Mr. Dock Grasser. Is there more than one boat trying to perform this trick?"

"I sure the hell hope not, sir. Grab the first slip you come to on your port side as you enter."

"This is MY MISTAKE. Sir, would you repeat, please! Also try and hang on to any slips of paper we need to fill out until after we get tied up."

The dockmaster combed his eyebrows with his little finger and looked at his helper and asked, " A. Kisser, what is that idiot talking about?"

"I don't know, boss, I haven't had much experience talking to idiots until I came to work here."

The dockmaster had a feeling there was more to that answer than meets the ear.

Anyway, coming in sideways put MY MISTAKE directly in line with the port slip. Bilge and Betty, seeing this miracle of being lined up with the slip, slammed both engines in reverse at the same time and killed them. Then the wind and tide blew them into the slip perfectly. Betty rushed to the bow, ready with a tightly coiled line in hand while Bilge was trying to get up enough nerve to start the engines again. Little lights and voices kept going off in his head saying 'quit while you are ahead fool'.

The dockmaster called to Betty, "Throw me the line, lady."

And Betty did . . . the whole thing.

There he stood with the line draped over him like a Christmas tree wreath. "I didn't mean the whole thing, lady, I just meant the end."

Betty instructed, "You didn't say the end, sir. I distinctly heard you say 'throw me the line'."

Hands on hips, the Gay-One quipped, "When I said, throw

me the line. That did not mean the whole thing, sweety."

Panicking like a good husband should, Bilge yelled, "Betty! The boat is floating away. Do something quick!"

"I am, Bilge. I'm trying to get this complaint handled as soon as I can."

Meanwhile, MY MISTAKE was drifting to the other side of the slip. Their future neighbors were lined up trying to fend off the approaching vessel.

"Now, sir," Betty said, "back to what we were talking about."

On the verge of pulling his hair out, the dockmaster surrendered. "You win, lady. I'm going to throw you the end of the line. You place the eye on the bit."

The dockmaster heaved away and Betty caught the end in a bear hug. "Okay, lady, now that you have the line, I want you to make it fast."

Betty abruptly stopped. She stomped her foot and squinted her eyes. She angrily asked, "Sir, who are you? And what right do you have to tell me to hurry up? I consider that rude!"

"Ma'am, I'm not trying to tell you to hurry up. I just want you to make it fast, please!"

"Well, I never! Begging won't rush me one bit, mister! That doesn't even work for my husband."

Meanwhile Bilge was yelling, "Betty, if you don't do something quick, I'm going to killllll yoooouuuuuu."

Betty turned toward her husband and squealed, "Bilge, you stop acting like somebody else's husband.

"Okay, Mr. Rude Dock, what do you want me to do with this string?"

Meanwhile, the neighbors were helping the dockmaster with his predicament. One of them yelled, "Tie the damn thing up and quit picking on the lady before you wreck our boats."

Another friendly neighbor added, "What the hell are you dock guys good for besides riding around on golf carts looking for tips? For chrissakes, be some help to the lady."

After receiving all the friendly advice, the dockmaster begged, "Ma'am, I'm sorry. Please tie the string to the little thing on the deck with the small horns."

"That's much better, sir. Politeness while complaining is a far better approach. Remember, when people you are complaining to, think you are sorry you are complaining about what you should be complaining about, they are far more receptive, even if they don't think you should be com . . . ."

"Beeeettttttyyyy, you're going to die soooooon if you don't tie that damn thing to something."

Betty thought, husbands, @#$%%$#@$#%."

"Okay, tie the string to what, Mr. Queer-One ?"

"To the bit, pleasssse, lady."

"Bit of what? You said, tie it to the little thing with the horns. You don't have to humor me, Mr. Queer. I know that the little thing on the deck is the compass."

At this point the dockmaster would have been glad to agree to anything. His boss just arrived to investigate the problem. Gay-One said, "Okay, lady, tie the line to the little horny compass on the deck. That's right, wrap the hell out of it. We have a big axe. We can get that knot loose later."

Mr. Daily Sufferer had a strange look on his face while Gay-One was pulling MY MISTAKE's bow to the pier. He asked the dockmaster, "Gay-One, have you been spending too much time in the men's dressing room? Did I hear you tell that lady to tie the line to the compass?"

"Boss, for the sake of our marina's future, trust me."

Meanwhile, there was more helpful advice from the neighbors.

"For chrissake, don't stand there talking. Get the stern in. Does the lady have to tell you guys how to do everything?"

Bilge was helping like a good husband should. After the engines were turned off, he remained on the flying bridge to take care of the yelling and panicking – the God-given right of all husbands, who become captain by right of birth.

The assistant to the assistant dockmaster said, "Lady, throw me the end of the line."

She did.

"Not that end, ma'am. The one with the eye."

Betty examined the line very closely and said, "Young man, I don't see any eye on this line."

"Lady, it's the one with the loop tied in it."

"Then, why didn't you say, 'throw me the end of the line with the loop in it'? If you are going to use nautical-legalizing that requires multiple answer questions, please decide which one of the multiple answers you want to your questions."

"I understand, lady. My new parole officer talks the same way. He used to work for the IRS."

Anyway, they finally got good ole MY MISTAKE tied up. The dockmaster shook his head and grumbled, "This is the first time I tied up a boat in spite of the owner."

His boss remarked, "Gay-One, you have to learn to be patient with people. Get involved with their problems. Show them you care and learn to put their stupid remarks to work. Now watch me make friends and handle this party."

Bilge was peering off the back of the boat making sure the Little Boat was safe, when the boss asked, "Sir, I heard you had trouble with your dinghy this morning." Betty approached and overheard Mr. Sufferer add, "Do you like how your dinghy works? And do you and your wife think it's big enough to do the job?"

Betty squealed, "Well, I never! What a disgusting man! How dare you ask a question like that!"

"Lady, I didn't mean any harm. I was just asking your husband whether you like his dinghy and whether it is big enough."

"I heard you ... you south end of a northbound horse. I declare, you should have your mouth washed out with bilge cleaner."

The dockmaster was grinning like a dog passing a peach seed and wondering whether he woke up on the right planet this morning.

Mr. Sufferer asked, "What did I say, for Godsakes?"

"Sir, the size of my husband's dinghy and whether I like it or not, is none of your sex crazed business."

Mr. Daily Sufferer begged, "Someone help me out of this idiotic mess!"

Ahha! The dockmaster's opportunity for revenge! "Boss, talk to my assistant's assistant. He said that he's learned a lot about talking to idiots since he started to work here."

The assistant, attempting a glow of innocence, said, "I

didn't mean it the way it sounded, boss."

"We'll see, dummy. If you don't handle this idiot, I'll think you meant me! And that, wise guy, will be the end of your work release."

The assistant to the assistant said, "Mr. Gay-One, I think you should . . ."

Mr. Sufferer snapped, "Not that idiot, you idiot. The ones on the boat."

The assistant to the assistant relying on the way he handles his parole officer, mother, grandmother, and especially his stepfather, said, "Ma'am, you are soooo right. All these people don't seem to want to understand the right way to say things, cause when the right thing is said, everybody understands what to say even if the other person doesn't know the right way to say it and even though the boss was trying to say the right thing, you are right, ma'am." He almost added, now can I use the car?

[THIS LINE WORKED BEST ON HIS SENILE GRANDMOTHER, BUT HE NOW HAD BETTY AND EVERYBODY ELSE NODDING THEIR HEADS AND WE KNOW WHAT THAT MEANS.]

Bilge knew the boy was right. Betty asked, "What in the pooty pot does that mean?

Following the policy of a smart boss, Mr. Sufferer got the hell away before anyone could ask another question.

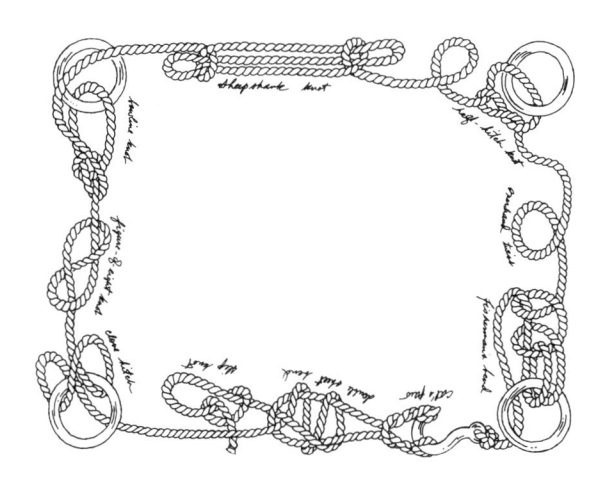

86

# CHAPTER EIGHT

Before the two sailors could take a well-earned tinkle or admire their good work of tying up, over she came. With an over expressed lyrical voice she announced, "Helllooooo to yooouuuuu. I hear you are the Scuppers. How nice. I knew your Uncle Side Scuppers, so you have to be nice, too. I only know nice people, of course. My name is Princess Busybody and this is my husband, Bigboat Bigshot. Our boat is the big, big new one on the port side of you, called, of course, THE PRINCESS CHOICE. We just came over to say, welcome, welcome, welcome. We were friends of your uncle for a long time. If we can help you in any way, all you have to do is ask."

Bilge thought, I don't believe that crap. If I ask her type for a favor, she'll get amnesia.

Bigshot shook hands with Bilge and said, "Our boat is the one next to yours but don't think we are boat snobs even if yours is not nearly as big or as new as ours."

Bilge was wondering if kiss-my-god-damn-smaller-boat-ass would fit this situation. Not sweet Betty. She thought that the Princess was so genteel as every piece of jewelry the Princess owned flashed in the morning sunlight.

Betty said, "We are so glad to meet you, especially since you knew our uncle before he was nice enough to die and leave us this boat. I'm so excited . . . We're going to have so much to talk about."

Ole Bigshot said, "Well, Bilge, I hear you are new at the boat game. Don't worry. You have it made, fella. I'll be glad to tell you aalllll about my vast experiences and that should help you a lot."

Bilge thought, yeah, right before I need to be bored to sleep.

Princess Busybody chimed in, "Betty, quick . . . don't look. Here comes your other neighbor with another one of his many nieces. Look at that skimpy bathing suit she's wearing. I wouldn't be caught dead in something like that."

Bilge was trying to get his glasses back on. His eyeballs

popped out after one quick look at that broad's T-back bathing suit.

Betty scolded, "Bilge, it's terrible to see a grown man look like he's about to foam at the mouth. Now you stop it before you embarrass that young lady."

Ole Bilge was thinking, the last time that little niece got embarrassed was when she ran out of hand oil at the massage parlor and had to rough it.

Princess Busybody was dragging Bigshot away. He was going cross-eyed trying to see the niece from the corner of his eye.

Meanwhile, the neighbors in discussion on the starboard side were heading their way.

Bilge thought to himself, hell, ole buddy, if you're going to take a look, take one. You're going to catch just as much hell for a little one as a big one.

The starboard side neighbors arrived just in time to receive a dirty look from the Princess. You could tell immediately that the two neighbors disliked each other. The approaching neighbor was about 5'4" with an oversized toupee and wore a T-shirt stating modestly, "I'm the main stud". He was accompanied by a centerfold candidate wearing the closest thing to indecent exposure that could be called a bathing suit.

"Hello, neighbor. My name is Charlie Try-Em-All and this is my niece, Miss Goodies. I see you already met the Princ'Ass and Big'Shit."

Betty politely corrected, "Oh, sir, I think you said their names wrong."

"Wait till you get to know them, lady. Then you'll think I'm too kind. Did he start telling you about his vast boating experiences yet? No? Well, just wait. That experienced sailor has to hire a captain to go to the fuel dock."

Betty inquired, "Mr. Tylenol, you must have a lot of experiences to talk about, too."

"Cute little lady, my niece and I have had some very interesting trips on my boat. Not only that, but I took a lot of close-ups of my action as mementoes. When you and your husband have a little time to see my close-ups, I'm sure you'll enjoy our action."

After the neighbors left, Betty said, "Bilge, don't you think that man was soooo nice to let us share his experiences on boats? Bilge! What's wrong? What are you thinking? You have that same naughty look on your face as the time that man at the store tried to sell you those dirty girlie books."

Bilge thought, women always think they know what's going on in a man's mind by the look on his face.

Betty read his mind like all wives can and said, "YES!"

---

Vrrroooooooommmmm . . . Vrrroooooooommmmm . . . Bamp . . . Bamp..BAMMMMMMMMMMMMMMP . . . "1-2-3-testing, 1-2-3 testing!"

All eyes were drawn to the slip in the back of MY MISTAKE. In that slip was a beautiful, 65-foot sportsfisherman with every possible gadget imaginable on it. The boat had a tuna tower with 3 decks, outriggers, multi controls, two different types of radars. You name it, this boy had it. And if it was about to hit the market, he had it ordered.

Ole Voom Voom Testing was waving at his new neighbors. He gave them and the rest of the marina just what he thought they needed, another round of "vroooom . . . vroooom" from his engines. He started his "testing, testing" bullshit all over again and a loud BBBBBBBBBAAAAMMMMMMMP on his horn.

After the Scuppers finished waving at Voom Voom which made his day, Betty asked, "Bilge, honey, who are those strange looking people in the slip across the way?"

"His wife is cute, Betty, but from the looks of the husband I don't think he has both oars in the water."

Betty called, "Yoooooo hoooooo, Princess Busybody. Who are those people on the boat called SABBATICAL across the way?"

"Betty, that's the Know-It-Alls. She is nice, but the husband's a smart ass writer type. Stay away from him."

Betty said, "Bilge, my sweet old port-side portly, I think the best way to get to know our friends is to have a little party at sundowners."

Bilge replied, "That's a great idea, little ole starboard side cutie."

The "ole" part of his statement got Bilge a warning look from Betty and he added, "But I don't think our neighbors like each other. But, I have a good idea that will get them all here."

Bilge went over to Bigshot who was admiring his own boat and looking down his nose at the rest of his neighbors. Bilge said, "Hi, Bigshot. How would you and your wife like to come over to a little sundowners get together so we can get to know our neighbors?"

"Is Charlie Try-Em-All and one of his nieces going to be there?"

"Why yes, why do you ask?"

"If that dipstick is going, I'm not."

"That's strange, Bigshot. The reason he said he was coming is because he knew that you wouldn't come. He also said that you don't have the macho to try and stand out around him."

"He did! Crap on that horny old bastard. I'll bet he's using popsicle sticks wrapped with rubber bands as a splint to make his thing stiff. We're coming. What time? Bilge, do me a little favor. Leave that writer on the SABBATICAL out. He's really not one of our type. He's not top drawer... if you know what I mean. All those writers have the easiest job in the world; they just sit on their asses and make up stories."

"Seven on the bow, Bigshot. Make no mistake. It's on MY MISTAKE."

Ole Bilge was using some of the same stuff that got him to the top in ladies' underwear. He remembered a technique that never failed with the ladies. Tell them that someone else has it and that they can't have it, then, watch what happens.

Anyway, Bilge knocked real hard on Charlie Try-Em-All's boat. Charlie emerged, worn-out, half-dressed, zipping up his pants and asked, "What can I do for you, Bilge? By the way, thanks for the break."

"Charlie, how would you and one of your nieces like to

come to our sundowners party?"

Charlie pointed toward BigBoat Bigshot's boat and asked, "Is Big Pile of Shit and his nosy wife coming?"

"Why yes, Charlie. He said he would come and you wouldn't because you are jealous of his abilities as a lover."

"Me, jealous of him? With that bow wow he has for a wife? The last time that old fart had it up, he was standing on his head. What time? I'm coming. Bilge, don't ask that writer will you? He'll copy down every damn thing we say."

"Seven on the bow and bring your cute little bow wow wing-dinger." Bilge heard a little voice call, "Charlie, it's getting cold."

Bilge headed for Voom Voom's boat and started yelling his head off trying to get ole Voom Voom to hear him. When Voom Voom shut the motors off, Bilge was still hollering at the top of his lungs.

"VOOM VOOM! Do you want to come to our sundowners party?"

"Bilge, you shouldn't holler like that. People around the marina don't like people who make a lot of noise. I don't think we can come, anyway. I saw you asking Charlie and since my wife, Miss Straight-Lace doesn't like Charlie's type, I don't think we can come."

Miss Straight-Lace emerged from the salon, nose pointed in the air, hair combed like Jackie Kennedy, and with a tight-ass New England accent she said, "We would like to come . . . darling . . . but you know how it is . . . we're so overwhelmed with our social calendar. Anyway darling, Charlie is one of those . . . Oh, you know what I mean."

Bilge said, "That's too bad. Charlie Try-Em-All said that he didn't think you would mind Miss Goodies, but he was sure you wouldn't want the Princess to outclass you."

"Where and when? We'll be there, Bilge . . . darling . . . don't ask that writer to come. Writers are so much like agents and editors. No class, if you know what I mean."

Bilge smiled at his success. "MY MISTAKE on the bow at seven."

Bilge returned to Betty to tell her of his success in getting everybody to come to the party.

Bilge said, "Little wife, I know you love having parties. But why, like most women, do you have to become a nervous wreck because you're having one?"

Betty thought, men, yuck! They don't understand anything.

She asked, "Bilge, what are we going to do about that writer and his wife over there?"

"I don't know, Betty. To get his sweet wife to come, we're going to have to put up with that old fool, too. Betty, you go over and ask them."

Betty walked over to the SABBATICAL and called, "Yoooo hooooo, Mr. Writer Man and your nice wife. Yoooo hooooo. Would you like to come to our party on the bow at seven? I know you already know everybody and maybe us. It would still be nice to have your wife at the party."

"Betty, I'm too busy to be bothered with going to a party."

"That's what we all thought you would say. They told me that you say stinky things about people in your books for not being good seamen and that you would be afraid to face us real sailors with your sweet wife watching over you. So there!"

"Hi, Betty. I'm Positively Know-It-All, this old grouch's wife. Don't worry, darling, we girls have to stick together. We'll be there, darling. Would you like us to bring anything?"

"Oh, just bring yourself, Mrs. Positive." Betty started to say 'and leave your grouch at home'... then thought she'd better not.

Mr. Know-It-All thought, the next book that I write is going to be a murder mystery, so I can enjoy killing this bunch off.

# CHAPTER NINE

Princess Busybody arrived at the party first. That snoopy broad would die if she missed anything. An early appearance also gave her a chance to set up her crucifixion line for the late arrivals. As always, the Princess was wearing every piece of jewelry, real or otherwise, that she owned. She wore the latest fashions whether or not they looked good on her and, of course, she smelled like a Macy's cosmetic counter. The last time she got in the condo elevator they had to call 911 rescue squad, to revive two old men who were riding with her.

Bigboat Bigshot was playing it low key in dress this night: bright red sports coat, red slacks with a white nautical belt, green shirt with white suspenders. One of these "play it safe" kind of guys. He smelled like bargain day at the Brut factory.

Princess said, "Betty, here come the Know-It-Alls. I don't see what that sweet girl sees in that old grouch. Did you hear about his background? I have it from a good sorted source that he was involved in a lot of cloak-and-dagger stuff, all kind of war things, and union strikes."

Betty asked, "Princess, you mean he was a fat Clint Eastwood?"

"No, darling, more like a pudgy roly-poly 007."

"I hear she comes from a very good family who hates his guts. It's sure easy to see why. The way he writes all that stuff about us, you would think we were like normal people or other such low types. Betty, you know I just loooovvvvve Positively and would never say anything about her, but . . . I don't see how she always keeps her cute figure. I've wonder how she does it? Another thing I can't see is why that man doesn't give me a starring role in this book, I'm sooooo interesting, darling . . . and my past . . so much to tell!"

Princess added, "Shhhh, here they come. We better not let him think we are talking about him. He thinks everybody is a character and that he can say anything he wants. The nerve of that man."

Positively said as she dragged Know-It-All aboard, "Hi

Betty, and you too, Princess. I came over to help you with the party. I promise to make Mr. Know-It-All keep his mouth shut."

Mr. Know-It-All said, "I'm glad to keep my mouth shut. Talking to this bunch makes as much sense as tinkling in the air and yelling it's raining. So punish me and I'll go home and watch Miami lose. I have no intention of forgiving Betty for having a party on the same night as "Monday Night Football"."

Princess whispered, "Watch it! Everybody, here comes Straightlace. Oh God! She's bringing those sailboat persons aboard. For Pete's sake, look at that dress Straightlace is wearing. I'm sure it's a GoodWill Industry special. Don't tell her I told you, but I heard it from a sick friend of mine that she used to be one of Charlie's nieces."

Straightlace and Voom Voom arrived wearing their best plastic smiles followed by two people dressed like Popeye and Olive Oyl. Straightlace was mad as hell at Voom Voom for making her late and allowing Princess to get in the first licks.

Ole Voom wore everything sold in a boat store and then some. Miss Straightlace was dressed as usual in a black, straight, long skirt and a white lace, high neck blouse with everything fitting tight as hell. Her perfume smelled like Lysol.

As they were coming aboard, Betty said, "Princess, I didn't know Charlie was old enough to have a niece her age."

"Not that kind of niece, Betty. You know what I mean."

Betty was nodding her head and asked, "I do?"

"Sure you do, darling. I will tell you a lot more about her another time."

Well Miss Straightlace and Voom arrived . . . to what else? . . . The Princess saying, "Daaaarling, I'm so glad to see yooooouuuu. I was hoping you and Voom Voom would come. It was so nice of Betty and Bilge to invite all of us."

"You are so right, Princess." Straightlace added with an acid smile, "I know you're looking forward to seeing Charlie since you two got along so well at the last party. Betty darling, I hope you don't mind that I brought along my dear friends, even if they do own a sailboat. This is Portly Port Tack and his longtime friend Ms. Jib Sheets. Even more important, she's one of his screws, I mean crew."

Betty greeted, "Oh, I'm glad you brought them along, Miss Lacey Pants. Any friend of a big blow is a friend of mine. We're definitely charmed at meeting you, Mr. Pott Racks, and you too, Ms. Jib Shits."

With her sour masculine voice, "It's Jib Sheets, darling, not Jib Shits."

"Oh, I'm sorry about your shits, but we are still charmed."

Princess icily asked, "Is that a new dress you're wearing, Straightlace, or is it the weight you gained that makes it look so, you know, so tight and sexy?"

Ignoring Princess' remarks, Miss Straightlace said, "Hello, Captain Scupperrs. You too, darling Betty. I just love that little red and white striped sundress you're wearing."

Betty looked like a mid-channel racing marker. Bilge's day was made, call him "captain" and he'll follow you anywhere.

Ole Bilge shook Voom Voom's hand and said, "Those engines of yours sure sound great, Voom Voom, they sound like, real power." Bilge knowingly made a friend for life.

Bilge reached out and shook Portly's hand vigorously. Portly was dressed like a fire plug with bell bottom trousers. His beard, bald head and pipe rounded out his facade.

But Bigshot was ready to take his shot. "Your engines sound good, Voom Voom. Too bad you don't go anywhere with them."

"Well, Bigshot, I would but I'd hate to hire a captain every time I take on fuel, like you do."

Bigshot answered with his best sick smile and inquired, "Voom Voom, what do you think about that billiard shot arrival that old Bilge made coming in? Bilge, I bet you were glad the wind was blowing in the right direction."

Bilge replied, "I was lucky with the wind. You know how it is, when you have a pretty face, everything turns out good. But I'm curious about something, Bigshot. I got a note from the dockman saying he would warn me when you took your boat out by yourself, that will give me ample time to hide my boat."

"I got the same note too, Bilge. Haaaaaaaa . . . Haa,"

snickered Voom Voom.

---

Meanwhile back with the girls . . .

Princess said, "Here comes Charlie Try-Em-All. God, look at that tight dress that so-called niece of his is wearing. I think her boobs are going to pop out any minute like beach balls from under the water."

Miss Goodies was wearing one of those convertible dresses. The front windshield was way down with an excellent view of her rear.

Straightlace complained, "I can't stand it when Charlie dresses like a teenager. He has more gold chains around his neck than a Sears jewelry counter."

Ole Charlie was wearing one of those 'anybody for tennis' outfits.

Positively said, "If that jerk falls overboard with all that iron around his neck, he's going straight to the bottom. I don't like Charlie, but my husband likes his late night naughty movies. Those two are definitely dirty old men."

The good ole boys were thinking the same thing about Miss Goodie's goodys popping out of her tight dress. In their case however, it was more like hoping.

"What do you think of Miss Goodies, Bilge?" asked ole Bigshot.

Bilge, was trying to get a good look at Miss Goodies goodys as she leaned over to pick up her handkerchief before coming aboard. He thought, it's strange how that kind of lady always seems to be dropping something. But as you know, there's always a wiseguy nearby who will ask an embarrassing question in front of your wife because he's too chicken shit to answer in front of his.

Bilge, after a little stammering, said, "Well, Bigshot, she appears to be a very intelligent young lady."

Mr. Know-it-all thought, I've used that one before, Bilge. I didn't get away with it, but I used it.

Betty warned, "Bilge, you have that strange hungry look

on your face. I don't like it when you use it on anybody else but me."

[BILGE GOT CAUGHT WITH A HORNY, OLD BUZZARD LOOK ON HIS FACE. HAVEN'T WE ALL?]

Princess mollycoddled her words, "Hello, Charlie. Nice to see you again." She did everything possible to make sure that she didn't acknowledge Miss Goodies' presence.

Jib Sheets greeted Charlie contemptuously, asking, "Been doing any midnight sailing lately, Charlie or just anchoring out for safety sake?"

Being a master at the smart ass game, Charlie responded, "I've been using the sheets lately if that's what you mean, Jib ole girl. But I have given up on the manly type of ladies."

Jib Sheets deadpanned, "Forget it, Charlie. Just forget it." Jib thought, the last time Charlie gave up on a female she was swinging in the gorilla cage. The only reason that old dick wagger anchored out is when he thinks some gal's husband can't swim.

Anyway, our Betty warmly greeted them, "Oh Miss Goodies, I'm so glad you and Charlie could come. It's nice to have someone young and pretty at my party."

Betty just made one friend and two mortal enemies.

"Thank you, ma'am, for inviting us, Mrs. Scuppers. Charlie and I have been so busy on the boat."

Straightlace quipped, "I bet you have. I'm glad you came, too. You should be a lot of help to Betty. Serving, that is."

Bigshot asked, "Bilge, old buddy, why in the hell did you let someone talk you into a wooden boat?"

"They didn't talk me into it, I got it for nothing. We had a convenient death in the family."

And Charlie said, "That's how Bigshot got to be a bigshot, Bilge. His grandfather conveniently died when he was still in college at the young age of 43. He was about to change his major for the twenty second time when he received the good news."

Ignoring Charlie, his favorite pastime, Bigshot said, "Well Bilge, that's the only way I would have a wooden boat and I wouldn't keep it long, believe me."

"Why, Bigshot?"

"Man, look at all the upkeep on a wooden boat. Fiberglass, man, that's the thing. No upkeep."

Bilge inquired, "You mean all those fiberglass boats in the boatyard weren't having anything done to them?"

"Wellll, a little thing here and there to keep them shiny."

Charlie got a chance to get in his licks. He had an idea who it was who called his wife and told her about a stag-party aboard his boat. The party was planned while the ladies were out of town and Bigshot wasn't invited.

Charlie said, "You see, Bilge, when the bottom of Bigshot's boat got all full of blisters, they charged him fifteen thousand bucks to take care of those little things that keep her shiny. He had a polite shit fit when The Sink and Sunk Boatyard gave him the bill, if you know what I mean."

Bigshot started to contemplate the charges for killing a smart-ass.

Everybody proceeded to the bow after getting in their opening nasty remarks.

[REMEMBER, EVERY PARTY THAT STARTS WELL ENDS BADLY AND. . . SOME THAT START BADLY GET WORSE.]

Betty was rushing back and forth making sure everybody had drinks and hors d'oeuvres. Princess thought, far be it for those lazy men to help with the party. But, in my case, I'm far too much a lady to be involved in such doings. I'd die before handing a drink to Straightlace without spilling it in her frozen lap.

The men were reminiscing about the good ole days when Betty spotted the evening "dock whatever" driving on the pier with a passenger in his golf cart. She found it odd that all the men quickly turned away and seemed to be looking for a place to hide.

Betty asked Miss Straightlace, "Who are those two men on the golf cart?"

"Oh God, Betty, one is Masculine Mealy-Mouth and that's Commodore Pompous-Ass. Get ready for his advice."

Commodore Pompous-Ass stepped from his golf cart assuming an air that everyone should kneel. He came aboard uninvited, put his hand out to the girls like some old stuffy bishop expecting his ring to be kissed.

He announced, "You must be Betty Scuppers. I've heard so much about you from your Uncle Side Scuppers. He was a real mariner, that Side Scuppers. One of the old class of seamen, like myself. Not one of these new types who have no idea how to tie up their vessel properly. I personally give the marina management my sound advice as to how this place should be run, but they don't seem to care or carry out my perfect suggestions efficiently."

Betty knew this was poo poo. She hadn't seen her Uncle Side Scuppers in twenty years but she knew he was frightened of traveling aboard boats. He had his boat delivered to the next marina and drove his car there. Betty, being the girl she is, allowed old Commodore to pile up the BS.

"Mrs. Scuppers, it is so nice to meet you. Thank you, I will take some hors d'oeuvres and any old drink will do, as long as it is exactly one and three-quarter ounces of Chivas Regal, one-eighth teaspoon lemon juice, from the peeling, of course, and exactly three and a half ounces of Schwepps soda with two large ice cubes. Make sure the ice doesn't crackle in the glass, darling when you add a little pepper tip. But don't put yourself to any trouble just for me. And ignore my driver will you, can't have the working man or whatever, sharing our spoils, now can we."

"Oh, it won't be any trouble, Commodore Pompous-Ass-Ass."

"There is only one 'ass' in my name, Mrs. Scuppers." The Commodore had a bewildered look on his face as he tried to rationalize the correction of his name.

Betty accepted his correction. Pink-cheeked with embarrassment, she quickly proceeded to the bar and with her overexposed photostatic memory proceeded to fix the Commodore's drink. "Now let me see, three and a half ounces of soda or was it three and a half ounces of, just like me to get it backwards, three and a half ounces of scotch, three and half ice cubes, and one and a half ounces of lemon juice. Now, one-eighth ounce of what, pepper, that's it, I have some cayenne right here. Oops, oh well, that little extra amount of cayenne doesn't make that much difference, anyway."

She handed the Commodore his drink and in his benevolent pontifical manner he said, "Thank you, my child." This old boozer was one of those guys who liked to gulp his drinks. He took one big gulp of Betty's wingdinger. Smoke started to come out of his ears and tears fell from his eyes and nose. This didn't stop the boozer from drinking it. But, needless to say, she broke him of that gulping shit.

Anyway, ole Commodore headed for the bow to impart some of his instructions to the boys. After a few gasps he said, "Bilge, my son, I see you've been introduced to some of the lower elements," he looked down his nose at Charlie Try-Em-All and added, "such as Charlie Moon over there. As a favor to your Uncle Side Scuppers, I'm going to take you under my wing and make sure you're introduced to all the right types. We do have a top drawer class here at the A'ss marina, ole boy. And with your vast experience as a boatman, I'm sure you'll fit in quite nicely."

Bilge thought, yeah, the vast experience of two days of travel.

The Commodore addressed the men, "Have you noticed, gentlemen, how disorderly this marina is operated? I'd also like to call your attention to the fact that the rubbish is only picked up twice a day and the management has the disgusting habit of using brown, of all colors, instead of white garbage can liners. White is the better class. What? I would also like to point out that the rope on which the flag is raised over the marina is taking on a soiled appearance. And, the idea of flying the Canadian flag on some of the boats about the marina has to stop. They're coming down here in larger and larger gaggles every year. One would think they are as good as we better types of open minded liberals."

He turned to Portly and asked, "Have you had a meeting with the sailboat owners and acted on my request to have all the riggings either clattering in the same tempo or to be stretched in such a manner that they follow a more presentable and better class of nautical tune?"

From the look on Portly's face he was either suffering from a gas pain or was trying desperately to come up with a like answer.

The Commodore, not hesitating a moment for Portly's reply, continued, "I have quite an extensive list of concerns that I'm going to send around for signatures so we can get some action . . . especially on the dress code for the help around the marina. I'm starting a movement to have all the marina employees outfitted in white bell bottom trousers, blue and white striped hats, and English tammies with red pom poms. Give the old place some class, what?

"I don't want to give you gentlemen the idea that I'm the complaining type or wish to insist on everyone's boat facing the same direction, lights out at nine and things of that sort. Also we special types, the upper class, if you know what I mean, should be allowed to roam freely about the marina after nine."

Bigshot leaned against the rail, lifted his glass, and gave one of his standard liberal toasts. "Here's to us better types. I wonder what the poor people are doing tonight?"

Princess heard her husband's loud magnanimous toast and, always the liberal one with the poor in mind, called back, "Oh my dear, I hope it's not the same thing we're doing. It would take all the fun out of being rich, now wouldn't it?"

Commodore Pompous-Ass added, "Don't worry, darlings. They wouldn't know how to act like one of we better types at the club, now would they? The last time I was at one of their clubs they were having a good time talking to everybody, buying each other drinks, smiling and dancing. Even if they wanted to, they wouldn't be able to sit quietly and get stoned out of their minds while downgrading everybody at the club, like the good members of our class do. Now would they, darling? Well so long, my children, I have a list of things to point out to Masculine Mealy-Mouth before he or whatever he is goes off watch. Princess have you hired Masculine as your personal driver, I seem to see you together a lot lately?"

The Princess was thinking, I wonder who I could hire to drown this old fart. The Commodore leaned over while looking at Charlie with disdain and whispered into Bigshot's ear. Bigshot lifted one eyebrow and snickered. The Commodore departed MY MISTAKE, saluted the ensign, and heard toots and whistles fluttering in his empty head.

After he left, Bilge asked, "Charlie, who the hell is that? Does he own the marina?"

"Own the marina? That ole dip-shit doesn't even pay his dues on time."

"Then he must have one of the mini-ships around here."

"No way, Bilge," Bigshot answered. "He doesn't even own a boat. He's a member of the yacht club and is a monumental pain-in-the-ass to everyone that owns a boat. He spends all his time complaining about the people who own boats and how the marina should be run. But just have a party on a boat and he's the first guy there wearing a captain's suit."

Bilge exclaimed, "You mean you don't have to own a boat to belong to a yacht club?"

Charlie snickered, "No. All you have to do is to be somebody's friend or son, pay your dues late, and you're in. Yacht clubs are for good ole boys who are good ole boys and want to keep it that way. You're a member, aren't you, Bilge?"

"Yes Charlie, my uncle passed it on to us when he passed on. By the way, what do you get for your dues?"

Voom Voom said, "You pay five grand to join and one thousand a year for the right to spend your money at the club. Not only that, they tell you the minimum you have to spend over a certain period of time. Now, ain't that a deal?"

Mr. Know-It-All added, "But there is that other very important compensation, you get to wear nautical clothing whether or not you have a boat and be as much of a stuffed shirt as one can handle. I must say Bilge, if it weren't for a few good members that club would go to hell."

Bilge asked Charlie, "Why did he call you Charlie Moon?"

"Bilge, you see those condos over there? Well some of those people have binoculars and some even have telescopes and nothing better to do than spy on us down here on the boats and look for something to complain about. Sooooo, I decided to give them something to complain about. Sooooo, I moon them at five o'clock every day.

"That whole bunch said they never do any spying. Sooooo, one evening I had Miss Goodies give them a first-class moon. That's when the trouble started. You see all those people who said they never spied on boats became a crowd of one hundred and fifty old men with every kind of viewing device that could be had. They were lined up on the balconies waiting for the next Miss Goodies show. When Miss Goodies didn't turn up the next day and I did, they all went down to the office and complained to the management that the condo commandos were cheated of their rightful view. They claimed that they were shown some old cheap hairy ass second, instead of the real thing."

"Well, what do you think about Commodore Pompous-Ass, Bilge?" Voom Voom asked.

Bilge avoided what he was really thinking and said, "I personally think he's a great asset to the marina and I'm sure the management here appreciates his suggestions on how to run everything."

Betty and the girls joined the men on the bow and overheard Bilge's last statement. Betty asked, "Bilge, doesn't Commodore Popsicle remind you of that lady, oh, what's her name, who used to come into the store every week and complain?"

"I know who you mean, Betty. Ms. Chronic Pain-In-The-Ass. She's the same type, same personality, honey."

The Princess insisted, "We need the Commodore to keep out the low types and overcome the moonies."

Bilge said, "I don't know, Princess, and pardon me for saying it like this. But when he extended his hand, palm down, I didn't know whether to shake it, or he expected me to kiss his ring or kiss his ass."

"Bilge, you naughty boy. If I hear you talk dirty mouth, I'm going to fuss you good."

"Sorry, Betty."

Old Bigshot said, "Bilge, do you let her talk baby talk to you in front of friends? I don't go for that baby talk stuff myself."

The Princess was getting on load of booze and the bravado to go with it and quipped, "No snuckie pie, biggie biggie Bigshot darlin'. You never want mumsie to talk baby talk to you, do you?"

Old Bigshot was thinking, I've planned this broad's

murder a million times in my dreams. I wonder which one of my plans I can get away with?

Miss Straightlace asked, "Betty, it seems like Bilge always gives you your way. Is that . . . normal?"

"Well, Miss Straightjacket, I've discovered how to get my way with Bilge. You could either say something really sensible or nag the daylights out of him till he agrees. Of course, there's that other way." She received grins of acknowledgement and big catty smiles from all the females. Betty blushed, "Oh, not that, I mean cry first."

Suddenly MY MISTAKE began rocking. Everybody grabbed for something to hold on to as fast as they could. Princess gulped her drink before any could spill. When the waves from a boat leaving the marina subsided, Bilge asked, "Why does the guy driving that boat have to go so fast inside the harbor?"

Charlie said, "That's one of those young boat jocks. They drive a boat like they screw, fast and noisy, or they think they aren't doing it right. Just think. If they ever slowed down, they would enjoy the ride, if you boys know what I mean."

"Disgusting men. Bilge, that's a naughty grin."

The party continued with its normal sarcastic, nasty, little innuendoes until the food was gone and the booze was increased. Then the girls sharpened their claws and really got nasty and the good ole boys became very nautical.

Old Bigshot was giving everyone lessons in celestial navigation. "Now you take that star over there on the left. That's really identified as the Stella Polaris or the North Star. You can always tell where you are as long as you can locate that particular star. It is the most important one in the heavens for us, experienced sailors. I'd say it's the most stationary of all the stars. Excuse me, gang. I've got to go down to the head for a moment. I'll be right back."

When old Bigshot returned he received condolences from Betty. "Bigshoots, something happened to your star."

"What? What are you talking about, girl?"

"You know that star on the left you were pointing to, the stationary one?"

"Yeah, what the hell's going on? There must be a cloud in front of it."

"Not really, Biggitshots," Betty replied as sweet as she could. "Your star just passed over with flashing red lights and made a plop-plop-plop sound. Does it pass this way every night so we know where it is? Or, where it is, we are?"

Charlie Try-Em-All had an 'I'm glad I got rid of that gas' smile on his face. Voom Voom's look was easy to read. It said, 'you deserve it Bigshot, you show-off craphead.' And ole Bilge wanted to kiss Betty.

Princess was going to get even for her husband and asked, "Betty, do you have much experience identifying stars? It seems you can recognize a real one from a phony."

Betty said meekly, "The only experience I've had with stars, is one time I thought a real star came to my department. A man who looked just like Robert Redford came in and made a complaint about his lawnmower not starting. I told him to put gas in it and look for something that said 'start' and pull it or push it. That's what I was told makes them go, I think. He was a nice man and thanked me very nicely for nothing. The way he said `Thanks for nothing, Charlotte. Personally, I don't give a damn anymore'. That made me think it was him. But my assistant, Miss Dim-Wit said that she didn't think it was him, because his hair didn't fall in his eyes."

After that, no one wanted to go any further with the star gazing.

[ME NEITHER AND I'M WRITING THIS BULL SHIT.]

Portly said, "Look Bigshot. Here comes a dingy from one of those sailboats anchored in the lake."

"Damn, you're right. There goes all the crap paper and soap from the shower room."

Bilge asked, "What do you guys mean?"

Portly answered, "Those lower type of sailboat people who can't afford a lofty position at the marina like us, dinghy in to take a decent crap and a bath for a change. Then they swipe all the soap and toilet paper. Nice people, don't you think? Definitely not top drawer."

And Betty said, "I noticed they were very rude when we passed them on the way up here just because Bilge was using both sides of the channel."

Jib Sheets butted in, "That's because darling, some of us

sailboaters and rightly so, think Christ used a sailboat on the Sea of Galilee. We still have the opinion that He travels with each one of us godly masters of the wind."

Charlie replied, "It's okay for you sailboaters to act like God is traveling with you but just try not to act like you're God when you're traveling."

And Jib Sheets asked, "Charlie, do I detect a little note of bitterness in your voice?"

"Damn right. Everybody writes books about you little gods on sailboats and never about us bigger lords on powerboats."

And, Princess said, "Mr. Know-It-All is writing a book about powerboaters, as you know. Some of us are the real stars in it."

Bigshot, showing the effects of his drinking, said, "If it wasn't for his wife watching everything he said, all of us would turn out to be a bunch of nuts instead of us typical, motor yacht, better type of people."

Mr. Know-It-All thought, I'll get that sucker for that remark, but I bet my wife will edit it out.

Anyway, after the star trip and the crap paper caper, the boys moved off to indulge in good ole men stuff like telling dirty jokes. The girls returned to the main salon and proceeded to rip each other apart.

Bigboat Bigshot started his "how do you like marriage" routine. "Well, Charlie, I see you're still getting away with that niece act. I thought you were going to get a divorce."

Charlie said, "Weellll, I like the idea of divorcing my wife, Brunhilder Stormtrooper but I couldn't stand the idea of being separated from her father's money." Lots of ha ha's from the men.

Bilge asked, "What do you think about marriage, Portly?"

"I don't. Because the sea to me, is like a green pasture filled with many cows and I am aboard my trusty steed of a sailboat rounding up the young heifers." He snickered and added, "Gentlemen, why should I buy one of those cows when I'm getting all this free milk?" Fortunately, the looks of envy on the rest of the men's faces were not being read by their wives.

Charlie asked, "What about you, Bigshot? Still getting your marriage counseling down at the ole massage parlor from Quick Hands Annie?"

Bigshot snapped, "That's none of your business. A man needs diversity. We're not like a woman who needs only one great man to dominate her life. Anyway, I consider marriage an institution and occasionally I feel that's where my wife belongs. My recommendations are, now mind you, I have the ladies' best interest at heart when I say this. They should be put on farms and used for breeding purposes and sport only and kept out of the mainstream of life. You know, be helpful to them, teach them to keep their mouth shut and say yes on time."

Mr. Know-It-All thought, for some reason my wife doesn't like this guy. I wonder what it is?

Bilge asked, "What about you, Voom Voom? You seem happily married."

Bigshot interceded, "Don't bother to ask. The boat is in his wife's name."

"What about you, Bilge?" Charlie asked.

"I have never felt married to Betty. It always seemed like we were one. I don't think of myself as half and her the other half. We're just one." For the first time Bilge got a new warm feeling after saying what he really felt.

Voom Voom said, "I don't have any marital problems. Me and my boat get along very well. I've adjusted to the fact that my wife is one of the minor accessories."

Meanwhile, back at the main salon. Princess said, "Straightlace, you and Charlie don't seem to be hitting it off tonight. Do you remember last New Year's Eve at the club? Some mighty close dancing, darling."

"Yessss, Charlie did come on a little strong so I had to put him in his place."

"Oh, is that what you call it?"

And Straightlace said, "What about you, Princess? That was quite a spectacle you put on over him, trying to cut in every few minutes. What is it with you, honey, trying to get into the niece business?"

Betty came to Princess's rescue. She didn't want anybody

to get their feelings hurt. She said, "Oh, I don't think Princess would want to be one of Charlie's nieces. She knows she is too old for such goings on."

If looks could kill, Betty would have been dead for two weeks.

And Miss Goodies said, "It looks like I'm not the only one trying to star in the niece business."

And Princess said, "The only stars you see, honey, are the ones painted on ceilings, right after payday." Princess broke the golden rule which is never to get into a pissing contest with a lady of the night.

Miss Goodies said, "Well, girls, anybody can give the damn stuff away. Remember, the older you get, the harder it is to put it out on consignment."

And darling, Betty said, "Give what away . . .?"

Miss Straightlace asked, "Goodies, have you ever thought of getting married instead of staying in your present occupation?"

"I would like to get married, but everybody who comes for my services is somebody's husband. So it makes it difficult to meet someone who's not married. Pardon me for saying this ladies, but if the son-of-a-b#$$#$%#$* is already no good and running around visiting whores, then let his wife keep him. And you, Miss Straightlace, are you enjoying your marriage?"

"Of course. A woman should take her prim and proper position in life and always maintain that attitude with a stiff upper lip regardless of how stupid and childish her husband is over his boat. That ugly rumor going around the marina that if the boat had breasts he'd give me up is a lie, I assure you. I'm more than willing to degrade myself in the sex act of marriage at least twice a year."

Princess was thinking, I know too much about you, babe, for you to sell that line to me. After that boozed-up statement which Straightlace would regret for the rest of her life, Princess couldn't wait for her chance to have marriage placed on its proper plane. The men joined the ladies as she was stating her opinion.

"I love being married, especially to a man like Bigboat

Bigshot. All women need a lord and master like I have. He's the type of man that let's you know you are a woman by his constant domination of everything you do. He reminds me how stupid we women are and that we should always rely on a man for everything important. My husband is one of those men who believes in the women's movement as long as it's their bowels. He allows me to buy whatever I want as long as I give him all the receipts with a lengthy explanation for each and every purchase. That includes the grocery bill and my hair appointment. He's so good to me."

"Betty asked, "Weeelllll, what's your opinion, Mr. Know-Nothing?"

"My opinion about what, Betty?" Mr. Know-It-All asked.

"About Bigshot."

"Hmmmmm . . . let me think about it. If my wife's not listening, I may adopt his philosophy."

Positively warned, "I am listening so you better not."

Betty asked, "Miss Jibbyjabby, what do you think about marriage?"

"It's Jib Sheets, darling, Jib Sheets. But to answer your question, I think marriage is a wonderful institution if one enjoys the idea of being incarcerated in an institution and preyed upon by male dominance and suffer the loss of being free to enjoy," she became misty- eyed, "the wind, the breaking seas over the bow, battling the elements, groping your way through foggy nights, the harrowing experiences of . . .! What the hell was I talking about?"

Ignoring her, Straightlace asked, "What about you, Betty, enjoying married life now that you're living aboard?"

"Weelllll, I don't know whether you could call it that anymore."

The witches were all ears.

"When we first got together I was very afraid of Bilge. I didn't know anything about men and he scared me a lot. My mother was a lot of help. She told me that she didn't think a girl like me could do any better even if he was not very smart or good looking. Of course, my sisters and aunts agreed with her, so I agreed to marry him. But I think he's soooooo handsome. Weellll, I was all wrong and so were they. He doesn't act like a mean man, except when he has to be for us; if you know what I mean. He takes care of me and makes me proud of him. That seems to be his main goal in life.

"But most of the time, he's just a little boy, who likes me to mommy him and he spends a lot of time trying to make me laugh. He feels perfectly content at being adopted instead of married. You know what he does when I am sometimes a little pooty to him? He says, `I'll apologize for you being a poot because I know in some way it's all my fault.'"

There were no dry eyes after that statement and the party ended.

---

Bilge and Betty sat on the bow discussing the evening's events. The sky was filled with stars and a soft gentle breeze blew off Lake Worth caressing them lovingly. In the distance, the lights flashed from an incoming vessel illuminating the gentle wave caps and reflecting off the full set of sails on an outgoing vessel for an evening on the water. Distant music from the club set the romantic scene for these two gentle souls to converse.

"Betty darling, your party was a grand success. The men went home drunk and full of friendship for each other until tomorrow and the girls went home hating each other more than ever. And Positively made her writer husband positively behave."

"Bilge, what are you thinking?"

"Oh Betty, I need a lot of people around me and all of them are you. You know what I mean. You don't have as much goodys as Miss Goodies, but you're better. You don't dress up like Princess who thinks she owns K-mart, but your dresses are prettier. You're not as phony, prim, and proper as Miss Straightlace, but you're so genteel. So you see, Betty, on this boat the only party I need is you. What are you thinking, Betty?"

"Bilge, I'm glad you're not a bigshot like you-know-who. And thank God, the only goodys you want to try are mine and you can vroom vroom your engines any time you want. And you know what else? I like that hungry, horny, naughty look on your face, fella, and I'm going to take you up on it right now."

**Off-shore Lifejacket**

**Near-Shore Buoyant Vest**

## A TYPE II PFD, or NEAR-SHORE BUOYANT

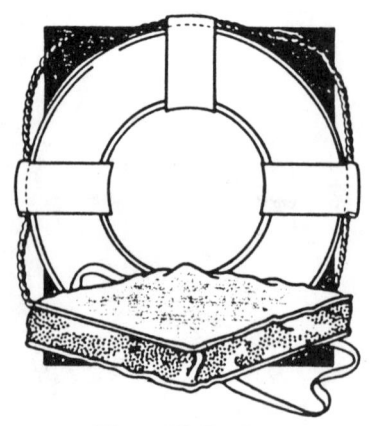

**Throwable Device**

**Flotation Aid**

# CHAPTER TEN

The next morning the two sweethearts woke up to the lovely sound of "Vrooooooom Vrooooooom. Testing 1-2-3, testing." Now for his second act of the day, Voom Voom turned on his radio [AND GUESS WHAT, FOLKS, I'M SURE YOU'VE HEARD IT A MILLION TIMES.] "This is Voom Voom on the Macho Machine for a radio check. Over. Wilco. Roger. Come in, please."

[BUT THERE ARE THOSE WHO DO NOT UNDERSTAND A CHILD LIKE VOOM VOOM WHO MUST PLAY WITH HIS TOY, NO MATTER WHAT IT IS.]

Some unknown bleeding soul answered his radio check, "The damn thing worked yesterday morning. It worked at noon. It worked last night before you went to bed. It works now, so give us a damn break, will you?"

Ole Voom Voom wasn't going to take that lying down on the flying bridge and he said, "I know who you are, spoiled sport, and I am going to tell your wife about those close-ups of Miss Goodies' moon trip you got from Charlie, so there."

Anyway, while the two grownups were having their little spat, the Scuppers were planning their next adventure.

"Bilge, it's going to be so informing to attend the Coast Guard class on Safety Afloat."

"Yeah, little sweetie bed-mate of more than one kind, if you know what I mean."

"Ooooooooohhh Bilge, you can say the most romantic things, but not so loud."

"Betty, I feel like screaming last night's doings all over this marina."

"If you do, I'm going to kill you, sweet baby."

---

[THE FOLLOWING ARE REAL QUESTIONS ASKED AT SAFETY BOATING CLASSES. I TOOK THE LIBERTY OF HAVING THEM ALL AT ONE CLASS.]

That night when the same class was arriving at the Power Squadron headquarters for the Coast Guard's instruction on Safety and Life Saving Afloat, most of the on-duty officers were trying to hide.

The class was called to attention.[THAT WOULD BE A GOOD TRICK.]

Attention was called by none other than the brand spanking new Ensign Precisely. He had the benefit of a thorough briefing by Commander May Day. The commander had told him, "Precisely, your career is on the line. The future of the service is in your hands. The safety of the American waterways is on your shoulders. Now go out there and try to teach the dumbest bunch of idiots ever to be assembled in one place how to keep from drowning each other. Always keep in mind that we must protect them from each other and in some way try to stay alive ourselves."

"You can count on me, sir. You know my record at the academy." As the Ensign walked away, the commander remembered the Ensign's record and started to pray.

Ensign Precisely mounted the platform in front of the class and said, "Fellow mariners, my name is Ensign Precisely. For short and to make things a little more personal, you may call me 'sir' at all times. Tonight we'll start with one of the most important and most misunderstood technological instruments on a vessel used for life saving . . . the life preserver.

"I say technological because I cover precisely what is precisely in the book. I was informed by some of your previous instructors," he almost called them cowards, "that this class had a slight amount of trouble with communications. When I deliver precisely what is in this book, you will have relatively few irrelevant questions because my communication will be precisely clear. Mariners, please feel free to take notes.

"Firstly, there are five types of PFD that the Coast Guard approves."

"Mr. Sir, my name is Half Whats-Going-On. I thought you said we are going to discuss life preservers."

And Ensign Precisely said, "We are discussing Personal

Flotation Devices."

And Half asked, "Then, does that make it precisely a life preserver?"

"Yes! As I was saying, there are five PFD. The first one is type 1. Type 1 PFD is designed to turn an unconscious person from a downward facing position in the water to a vertical or slightly backward position. It has 22 pounds of buoyancy. A type 1 PFD is, however, somewhat uncomfortable compared with the other types."

"Sir . . . ah, mister, sir. My name is Betty Scuppers. So I can make sure my notes are correct, how unconscious do you have to be when you put on Type 1?"

The hair rose up on the back of Ensign Precisely's neck. He said, "Ma'am, it is not necessary to be unconscious when you put on the life preserver. It is only if you become unconscious when you are in the water that Type 1 PFD is used.

"Next question, please."

"Sir, my name is Bilge Scuppers. I'm the lady's husband by marriage. For precise clarification, if you think you're going to be unconscious in the water, or for some other reason you are unconscious before you go into the water, are you recommending that we put on Type 1? Is that correct?"

"Mr. Scuppers, this has nothing to do with deciding to become unconscious." Ensign was thinking, this dummy is half unconscious as it is. "It is only used, class, when and if, you eventually become unconscious in the water.

"Next question, please."

"Sir, my name is Joey I Missed-Something. Type 1 is less comfortable than other types. Does that mean it don't last long enough?"

The nauseated look on Precisely's face was the only response he intended to give to that question.

"Sir, my name is Sadly What-The-Hell. I'm Joey's wife by default. What I want to know, and I'm sure every style-conscious lady wants to know, is Type 1 something I wouldn't be caught unconscious wearing?"

"Madam, I don't think anybody in this class has to be caught to be unconscious."

Ensign Precisely continued, "I guess I am forced to answer your interrupted question, Mr. I Missed-Something. You are precisely right and wrong about the lastability of Type 1."

"Oh," Joey I Missed-Something replied, "I understand that, sir. I'll read you back my notes to make sure that this is precisely what you expect. If I'm not unconscious and I do become unconscious and I weigh 20 pounds, I'm to wear this less comfortable life preserver even if it's the cheaper type . . . and Sadly won't like it 'cause it's out of style."

Ensign, turning a jaundiced yellow said, "Let me do this again. I'm sure you must have missed something. Type 1 is uncomfortable to wear but not completely uncomfortable, and it doesn't have a damn thing to do with cost or style."

"Yes, Mr. Half Whats-Going-On, you have something to add?"

"Yes, sir. If I'm unconscious, how am I to know whether I'm uncomfortable?"

Precisely stood with his mouth gaped open and managed to say, "Next question, please."

"Sir, my name is Always The Smart-Ass. There is a test that fella can take. He can hit himself on the head, put on the PFD, jump overboard and find out first hand. Haaahaaahaaaha!"

The Ensign thought, not a bad idea in this case.

Ole Half Whats-Going-On, a retired NFL linebacker who stood about six inches taller and one hundred pounds heavier than Smart-Ass, recommended, "I'm going to let you tell me all about that test, Smart-Ass, in the parking lot when class is over." This ex-bone crusher missed hurting people and he felt he had a great chance to break some bones without taking a scolding from his five-foot wife.

Smart-Ass got the pee scared out of him and went to take a leak. He ain't been heard of since.

While all this was going on, if one listened closely one could hear Lieutenant Blowhard and Commander May Day snickering with delight in the hall.

Ensign Precisely cleared his throat and said, "Let's move on to Type 2. Type 2 PFD is designed to turn an unconscious person up in the same manner as Type 1 and has at least 15 1/2 pounds of buoyancy. The Type 2 device is more comfortable for wearing than Type 1."

Betty reread her notes quietly and carefully because life saving equipment is very important. "Type 1 FTD... you can put on when you're unconscious and facing downward in the water so you can become backwards in your position and float for 22 pounds. But you will be uncomfortable when you're unconscious, so it's best to wear Type 2 FTD and float for 15 1/2 pounds and be comfortably unconscious."

To make sure she was correct, Betty showed her notes to Bilge. He agreed, but told her to be careful with her spelling.

Ensign Precisely continued, "Type 3 PFD is designed to keep a conscious person in a vertical or slightly backward position. It has 15 1/2 pounds of buoyancy. Note that Type 3 PFD has the same buoyancy as Type 2, but not the turning requirement or the protection for the person who becomes unconscious in the water. These factors make it possible to design a comfortable and wearable device for activities where it is especially desirable to wear a PFD in the event the wearer is likely to enter the water."

"Sir, my name is Pure D. What-The-Hell. We alls decided from your precise definition that we'uns gonna buy Type 3 'cause it's obvious you's a selling Type 3. I intend to be conscious and avoid bein' unconscious and I kinda' like a slightly laid-back position anyway, so I think the only thing lacking is it turning me around. Can I buy that as an extra? You also says this one's wearable, where them others ain't so wearable. So I think I'll get one of these for my brother-in-law, too. You can bet, mister, sooner or later that boy's gonna get drunk and fall into the pond. And like you done said, if the wearer is likely to enter the water, that is my drunken brother-in-law fo' sho'. He'll need one."

Ensign Precisely's blood pressure dropped to 12. He precisely said, "I did not intend anything of the kind!"

"Then, sir, why in the hell did you say it?"

"I didn't say it. I read it from this damn book."

"Who wrote that book, mister?"

"This book is issued by the United States Department of

Transportation. It lists the Coast Guard equipment items, approved, certified or accepted under the Marine Inspection and Navigation Laws. Now there, genius."
[THAT IS THE TRUTH.]
Ole Half Whats-Going-On asked, "Sir Precisely, is certified a different law than accepted or approved? 'Cause you said, approved, certified or accepted. Does this give us multiple choice life preservers? Is a certified one more comfortable than an approved one? And which one has the rack and pinion turning power?"

At this point Commander May Day and Lieutenant Blowhard were whopping with delight in the hallway as Ensign Precisely said, "Class, let's move on to Type 4. Type 4 is designed to be thrown to a person in the water and to be grasped rather than worn. It must have at least 16 1/2 pounds of buoyancy."

"Sir, my name is Mrs. Here For-Nothing. I don't own a boat but these classes are free and I don't have anything better to do with my time. Also, no one of importance died whose funeral I would enjoy and there are no weddings to attend. Not only that but "The Golden Girls" don't come on tonight so that's why I'm here in this class. To make this short, I would like to know how an unconscious person catches Type 4?"

Betty's notes read Type 4 FTD is used when a person is thrown overboard and is in the water, that is. To be specific, throw him a 16 1/2 pound buoyancy as he's gasping for breath.

Attempting to gain control of his sanity and the insanity of the class, Ensign Precisely proceeded undauntedly, "Type 5 PFD is any device designed for a specific and restricted use. Please go over your notes and read through your equipment list. Now I'm going to give you 15 minutes to familiarize yourself with your notes."

Ensign returned from the head where he was shaking so bad he was unable to pee.

Bilge was standing in the middle of the class as spokesman for the group and said, "Sir, I represent the unconscious consensus opinion of the class. We appreciate what you have taught us tonight and as you can see from our questions, we totally grasp the situation at hand. We intend to do whatever is necessary to improve safe boating."

Ensign Precisely heard Lieutenant Blowhard and Commander May Day yell, "If you really want to contribute to safe boating, the whole bunch of you dummies should sell your damn boats and move to Death Valley."

Bilge knew it was merely a pun, for no one would ever deny the sincerity of this class to become safe mariners.

[THESE ARE TRUE DESCRIPTIONS OF THE FIVE DIFFERENT TYPES OF APPROVED PERSONAL FLOTATION DEVICES. OVER THE COURSE OF MONTHS IT TOOK TO WRITE THIS BOOK, I HAVE CASUALLY ASKED 100 BOATERS TO DESCRIBE THE PURPOSE OR THE DIFFERENCES BETWEEN PERSONAL FLOTATION DEVICES. THE MAJORITY OF ANSWERS I RECEIVED WERE, "THE COAST GUARD REQUIRES YOU TO CARRY THEM" OR "THEY'RE GOOD FOR THE KIDS WHEN THEY WATER SKI". ISN'T THIS A FRIGHTENING STATE OF AFFAIRS?]

Ensign's voice was trembling as he pleaded, "Class, let's move from the topic of unconscious boaters both in and out of the water to another subject. I told you we had a special guest tonight, and here she is, Ms. Wildly Environmental. She is the head of 'Save The Earth For Everybody But The Society Of Man'."

Everyone applauded. They didn't know why they applauded, but, maybe it was because she looked as if she needed it.

She picked up the mike, turned it to maximum and said, "Can everybody hear me?"

The old man in the front row wearing a hearing aid had a circuit blow in his brain. As the old man tumbled to the floor, she said, "Oh, good, I'm glad everybody can hear me.

"Tonight I would like to alert you boaters about protecting the manatee. I am going to pass out these little yellow pamphlets which explain a number of cautionary and regulatory speed zones. The yellow color represents caution, of course. Oh, Mrs. Scuppers, it is so nice of you to volunteer to hand out the pamphlets." For some damn reason there was more applause. Everyone received a pamphlet plus a smile and a small curtsy from Betty. Bilge was thinking as he viewed the pamphlet that there was a striking resemblance between the guest speaker and the manatee pictured in the pamphlet.

Betty caught his look and gave a wifely warning, "If you laugh, you die, Bilge."

As the mike screeched, the opera singing manatee at the front of the class said, "Wooooonderfulll people, the pamphlet was designed to make it very easy for boaters to understand the different legal requirements for the safety of the manatee. There are six different signs or zones: (1) idle speed, (2) slow speed, (3) slow speed but you can go fast in the channel, (4) caution, (5) no entry, and (6) resume normal speed. Now if there are any questions just raise your hands."

The classroom looked like a forest of hands with waving fingers as leaves.

"Ma'am, I'm the same Half Whats-Going-On as before. How fast is idle speed?"

"It says it in your pamphlet. Idle speed zone is a zone in which boats are not permitted to go faster than necessary to be steered. These signs generally appear near the center of a protected sanctuary."

"Ma'am, I still don't know how fast that is. Do you go like hell until you get into the middle of those sanctuaries? Then lay-back and idle away on your boat? And do them critters know they are in the middle of the sanctuary or is it us that's in the middle?"

"That's a very good question. Now, let's move on to someone else."

"Bilge Scuppers, here. On the next two signs it says, Slow Speed Zone, a no wake or minimum wake zone where boats must be level in the water. These signs are generally posted on the fringes of protected areas to warn you that you are approaching an area frequented by manatees. But it says here, some channels are exempted.Ma'am, I would like to go over a few very good blunt spots on the points you are making. I've seen some of these boats running level with the water, making very little wake, and doing sixty-miles an hour. Let me be blunt about one more point. The signs are to warn you that manatees frequent these areas but channels are exempted. So now that you have warned some of those crazy boat jocks that they are exempted, all I can suggest, Madam Manatee, I mean, lady, is that you should make a sign for the manatee that reads, 'Duck Momma Manatee When You And The Kids Are In The Channel'. That sign should be under the water so that the manatee will know when they are in an exempted channel."

"Thank you, Mr. Scuppers, for blundering through those two pointed subjects.

"Yes, the gentleman sitting dazed in the middle of the class. What is your name?"

"Mr. What-The-Fusks, ma'am. I would like an explanation of 'caution' in a Caution Zone."

"If you are awake, sir, it says that it is a zone that is frequently inhabited by manatees and requires caution on the part of boaters to avoid disturbing or injuring the animals."

Mr. What-The-Fusks asked, "Does this mean that you can haul ass through the area as long as you miss them or not wake them up? Seems like there should be a sign saying, 'Slow Down Dummy and Make Damn Sure You Don't Hurt The Little Fellows'. And your next sign should say, 'Stay The Hell Out'. I think this would make more sense to a bit more people than, 'No Entry'."

"We'll take your suggestions under advisement for future study. I'm sure during our frequent luncheons and many banquets within the next four or five months we should be able to come up with at least half an explanation which I'm sure will require further studies."

"I'm the better half of the Half Whats-Going-On family. The next sign says: Resume Normal Safe Boating – Safe Operating Zone. This sign indicates you may resume safe speed, as you leave a protected area. Did I miss half the meaning or should it say, 'Watch Out For The Kids As You Leave The School Zone'? Sorry, I meant 'Manatee Area'?"

"All signs are not as clear as they could be, but some of us will understand. Now, won't we?"

"Ma'am, I'm Mr. May B. Bull S. Are you sure these are endangered animals? If there is one animal for every sign I see, there damn well are a lot of them. For instance, if there is one critter at every marina, one at every dock on the waterway and one for every boat moored along the waterway and one for every anchorage, there sure as hell are either a lot of manatees or a lot of liars who want to slow everybody down. If you overdo them signs, people are going to think they are being bull-poopooed and run over those little boogers for sure."

Ms. Wildly Environmental became defensive, "Sir, I hope you don't think we better types that live along the waterway are anything but fair in our dealings with boaters."

"You are right about that, lady. Some of you suckers are anything but fair."

Ensign Precisely thanked the guest speaker for enlightening the class and said, "Class, let's sum up. We have six different signs saying the same thing, 'Save The Manatee', but not necessarily saying it the same way. Thank you again for helping us, Ms. Wildly Environmental."

The class applauded as Ensign Precisely dismissed everyone for the evening. And headed for a bar to take his first steps in becoming a drunk.

# CHAPTER ELEVEN

That evening after class, Bilge was unable to sleep. He was deeply moved by the plight of the gentle manatee. Bilge walked to the bow as the light of the setting moon reflected its soft sorrowful mood upon the surface of the lake. As it dipped towards its tomorrow, the moon's glow increased the sadness welling within Bilge. He glanced on the surface and a ghostlike figure scattered the moonbeams. The silhouette of an old manatee called Crazy Nick appeared and said in a mournful voice, "Pray with me, Bilge. They call me Crazy Nick because I swim North in the winter. Wouldn't you humans who go skiing in the North be considered crazy, too?

"This is my prayer Bilge. Please, pass it along.

"Twelve hundred hopeful souls are we,
What is left of the gentle manatee
Has that bell tolled for such as we?
We're in the hands of man, you see
The rope is in the hands of man
Please stay this toll for as long as you can,
Oh, deathly bell, to your children you must tell
If you don't take a stand and save us when you can.
Who have we ever harmed,
As we swam along in these Florida seas?
But, many we have charmed throughout our whole life long
When have we ever caused an alarm?
Are there gentler ones than we,
That swim in sight so all can see.
Soon that bell will toll for me,
Oh, sorrowful bell, will your sad sound tell
The end of gentle me that swims in the Florida seas?
Man, listen close to that bell that tolls for me
Part of that bell will toll for thee
Please save us and never ring that bell.
Then on a happy note we can tell

It was man who stayed the bell."

---

Bilge thought, is this really happening? If Crazy Nick's prayer is real, I sure hope every boater hears it when he goes through a manatee area like a nut.

Nick resurfaced and said, "Sorry if I expected one of you humans to act like one of us, Bilge."

"It's okay, Nick. I hope we humans can learn to be as gentle as you are."

Betty came to the bow and asked, "Bilge, who were you talking to?"

"No one of any importance, Betty. Just daydreaming at night out loud."

A series of bubbles rose to the surface as Nick mumbled under the water, "I'll get you for that one, Bilge. So there."

---

Betty said, "Oh, Bilge, boating is so exciting. We are learning so many things not to do and how not to do them."

"Betty, let's have a little drinky poo and plan our future trip to the Keys."

"Bilge, when we have a drinky poo, don't you get horny poo again. You're getting to be such a fussy sexy doggy." With a naughty giggle, Betty hurried off to make the drinks.

When she returned, Bilge said, "Sweetie, I think we should get our oil changed before our grand adventure. We can go to the office the first chance we get and find out when they are free to do it."

"Look, Bilge. Here comes Bigshot and Princess taking their walk."

Princess said, "Helloooooooo, Betty, and you too, Bilge. My lord and master has an announcement to make that I'm sure will make you happy."

Bigshot announced, "Bilge, and your lesser half, haahaahaa, in retaliation for inviting us over I would like to take you kids to the club tomorrow night. I am sure you will find an evening with us uplifting and fun. I know everything about every restaurant and every good place to go. All you have to do is ask me."

"That's very nice of you, Bigshot, but . . . "

Betty said, "No buts, Bilge. Princess, we would loooovvveee to come."

Bigshot said, "It's a date; don't be late. We'll make it at eight."

Betty cooed, "Ooooohhhh, Bigshot, that sounds so romantic."

"I know, Betty. I always say the right thing."

After his Royal Butt-Face and Princess left, Bilge said, "Betty, why do you want to spend an evening with those two and listen to all that gossip? Well, I guess I answered my own question."

---

The next evening our two sailors were dressed in their newest and best. Bilge wore his black slacks, black open front blazer, a white shirt, a white vest and a black ascot.

[HE LOOKED LIKE A SAD, SUNBURNED PENGUIN.]

Betty, on the other hand, wore a full length yellow sundress with pink sequins. Her hair was frizzed out at all angles to fit the new bride of Frankenstein look. The striking couple met their royal butt-faces and proceeded to the yacht club.

The Princess wore a black fully sequined gown with all the doodads she owned, carried a white purse, and of course, she wore a small diamond tiara on her head.

Bigboat Bigshot, not a stand-out kind of guy, wore a bright red suit, open front green shirt and he had enough gold chains around his neck to anchor a ship.

The evening's soft breezes set into motion the gentle swaying of the palm trees. The bright moon reflected their images on the surface of the water. Betty was so happy, she started singing, "Moon Over Miami" in her squeaky little voice.

Bilge said, "It don't get no better than this unless you're in a beer commercial."

They were met at the door by the always present tight-ass constipated-looking maitre d'. He greeted, "Goooood eeevvvvening, sir. How many will there be this evening? Four? Well, that's nice. Your regular table, Mr. Bigshot?"

Bilge whispered to Betty, "I wonder what would happen if we said, 'not this evening. We came to wait for breakfast, and, yes, we would like Commodore Pompous-Ass' table so we could start some crap'."

"If you do, Bilge, I'll kill yoouuuuu."

The evening proceeded with Bigshot smiling and waving to everyone who entered the club. He wanted to be sure they would all remember that he had been there.

On the other hand, Princess and Betty were picking apart all the other ladies. "Do you see her? She's the one who was in one of those centerfolds. Now, you would think she was Sister Theresa but we know better, don't we? And the one with the white dress, she should be wearing black. She's already buried two husbands, and that one, she. . . ."

Ole Bilge noticed that all the women had light blue hair and were overweight and the men were dressed like they were going to a high school prom. After a flat tasting meal, boring music from the forties, and drinks that would knock your socks off, the evening was shattered by the appearance of His Majesty, Pompous-Ass himself.

"Weelllll, Bilge and Betty, I'm glad you could come and sample some of our high class company. It does one good to know you're among the best."

Bilge had one too many of those double drinks to put up with old Pompous-Ass' elevated crap. The boozers call those double drinks singles so they can say they don't drink much.Bilge slurred, "When are the better types supposed to arrive? And you know what, Commodore? The only way you could elevate this crowd is to pick them up with a manure shovel."

Commander Pompous-Ass tittered, "Bilge, you're such a joker. I'm glad no one takes you serious."

All this passed over Bigshot's head. He was busy dropping his napkin trying to look up one of the women's dresses at the bar. He asked, "Did you say something, Bilge?"

Betty came to the rescue and said with a glaring look towards Bilge, "He was only clowning around. Don't pay him any mind."

Bilge thought, have you ever noticed that no matter how focused a wife is in talking to someone else, she will hear her husband over a band and twenty people talking the first time he said anything wrong.

Bigshot asked, "Commodore, did I see some of the dock employees coming out of the club yesterday?"

"Yes, you did, Bigboat. We always do them a little favor by inviting them in to do some little old nasty job or other. Of course, we do lock up the beer tap and give them some of last night's leftover ginger ale. We can't let the working class think we don't care."

And Bilge said, "Why don't you kiss my working class ass. Betty, take your hand off my mouth."

"I will not! You are my husband and you aren't putting words in your mouth that belong in mine just because you're drunk enough to say them yourself."

Betty finally got Bilge to dance. There was something sobering about dancing with Betty. He loved the way she held him close, kissed his cheek and she gave a sigh every time he made a dip.

"Bilge, this is a wonderful evening. You're so romantic. Make sure you don't drink too much and spoil the late night performance."

---

The next morning after a very romantic evening Bilge was thinking about who the horny one was . . .

"Bilge, you stop thinking those kind of thoughts or I'll stomp my foot at you."

"Quit squinting your eyes at me, Betty sexy."

"Men are so disgusting, especially romantic husbands."

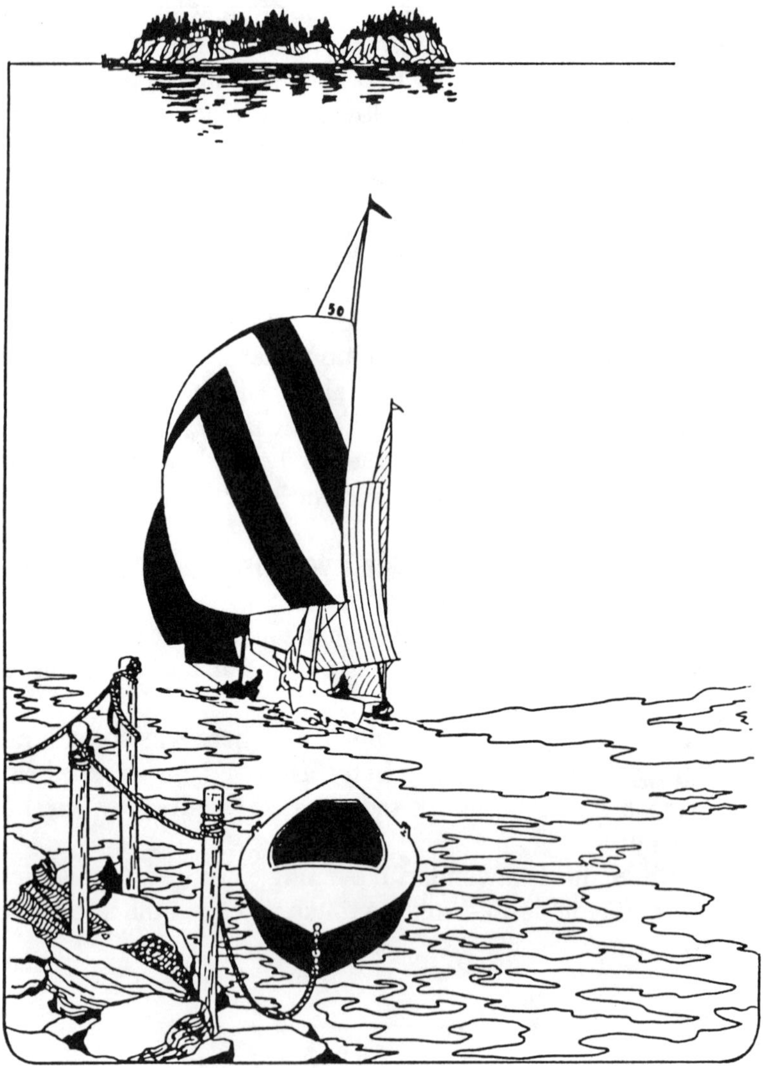
50

# CHAPTER TWELVE

Anyway, after rising the next morning and Bilge stating that only a bullet could cure his hangover, four cups of coffee later, and Betty being nervous as a wild cat with a sore behind, the two sweethearts headed to the office to arrange for an oil change.

"Good morning, everybody, I'm Mrs. Scuppers and husband. You must be Ding-A-Ling, you're so cute. I'll also say good morning to you, Mr. Dock Person, but not quite as nice."

Bilge said, "Good morning, Ding-A-Ling. It's a pleasure to meet your face at last."

"It's nice to see you too, Mr. Scuppers."

"All, you folks, can call me Bilge. Everybody seems to prefer using my first name when talking to me."

Ding-A-Ling said, "Bilge and Betty, this is Mr. Legal Bagel Barnacle. He has a habit of sticking his nose, sorry, I mean advising people of their rights around the complex."

Betty curtsied. Bilge shook hands and they both said, "We're charmed."

Legal Bagel Barnacle drew himself up to his full height of four-feet eleven-inches and was nearly that round. He offered, "My advice to you wonderful people, which is precious, is to watch these suckers in this office. Everybody thinks the manager is fair, honest, and reliable. When that happens, there is definitely something wrong. You see, that's what they say about politicians and they're crooked. I know for a fact because I was one myself. Now, I don't want to be longwinded but when your uncle . . . "

Ding-A-Ling came to the rescue, "Mr. Scuppers, was there something you wanted us to do for you?"

The manager walked in and Betty asked, "Mr. Management, what we would like to ask about, is what we would like to know, is . . . when would you be free to give us an oil change? Not for my husband and myself, of course. We can take care of that ourselves."

Bilge said, "Betty, watch what you're saying. It isn't coming out right."

"What?"

"Nothing, honey. Let it lie."

"Bilge, you're getting like that diggitty dog writer. When I say something right, you say I said something wrong." She continued, "Well, anyway, Mr. Suffering, when managing things, When?"

"When what?"

"When would you be free to give us an oil change?"

"We should be free to give you an oil change tomorrow morning, Mrs. Scuppers."

---

The following morning Betty was running around like a chicken with its head cut off, covering everything in sight with sheets, newspapers, towels, and anything else she could find.

[THE BOAT WAS WRAPPED AND APPEARED READY FOR MAILING.]

[WHEN MY WIFE GETS THE SABBATICAL READY FOR AN OIL CHANGE, UPS WOULD BE PROUD OF HER PACKING.]

When the mechanics arrived to change the oil, they were confronted by Betty. "Did you men wash your feet and are you wearing clean shoes? And, mister, you're not coming on my boat with those old clothes on."

"Ma'am, deys old, but deys clean."

Betty was unconvinced. "Maybe so, but I'm going to watch you close."

"We's got dat feeling right off, ma'am."

"What are those big buckets for?" Betty asked.

"Dats for the oil, ma'am. Two's full and one's empty."

Bilge asked, "Why the empty one?"

"So we have somethin' to puts the first oil we takes out of the first en'gine in."

After four more cups of coffee and still nervous, Betty panicked, "Oh, my God! Which one of my darlings are going to be first? Bilge, help me."

"Betty, I don't think it matters."

"Men! You are so cruel, you don't understand anything." Sniffle, sniffle.

"Don't cry, Betty. It's not going to hurt. It will feel good."

Betty stomped her foot and said, "That's what all you men say."

"Well, lady, we'uns are going to start with the generator first."

Betty squealed, "Don't you dare! You will frighten her. Start with the Big Boys first. And make sure you are gentle. I don't want them hurt."

Rufus Oils, one of the mechanics attempting to make the oil change, said to his buddy, "You know somethin', Greasy, I think these en'gines wasn't built . . . dat lady musta borne them."

"I's agree, Rufus, but whats you tryin' to tell me?"

"I's tryin' to tell ya, dat we's better watch ourselfs, cause dis lady ain't put her brain on dis morning."

Rufus replied, "I heard that."

Because these two oil jockeys had performed this task for the past twenty years everything turned out just fine.

---

After this oil ordeal, Bilge and Betty went to the office to get their mail.

Mr. Daily Sufferer said, "Mrs Scuppers, here's your bill for the oil change."

"My what?"

"The bill for your oil change. It's only three hundred dollars."

Betty stomped her foot and squinted her eyes. "You fibber, you stinky tail, you fakey person. Meowooooo, meowoooooo."

[THAT'S BETTY CRYING LIKE A CAT ON A BACK FENCE.]

The manager, near panic, asked, "What's wrong? What did I do wrong?"

Betty stomped her foot twice and squinted her eyes.

Bilge's bottom lip poked out as far as it would go and with his most threatening frown he said, "Sir, you said you were going to give us an oil change. Now your generosity has turn into poo. And our trust in you has vanished."

"Mr. Scuppers . . . "

"Call me Bilge until we get this straightened out and maybe then you will have to call me Mr. Scuppers."

Mr. Sufferer tried reasoning. "Bilge, 'to give you an oil change' is just a figure of speech. It costs money."

"Meowooooo, meowoooooo."

Guess who just walked in to help with the confusion?

"Commodore Pompous-Ass here. Bilge, I heard you met my good friend, Legal Bagel Barnacle. What's going on? Why are you making this lady cry, you half-rectum manager?"

The manager was thinking that if someone were going to piss in your soup, it might as well be horses. And here stood Legal Bagel and Commodore Pompous-Ass, two real horses' asses.

Betty put on her best 'poor Charlotte' act. "Dear Commodore Pompous-Ass, and maybe you too, Legal Bagel. I'm so glad you are here. My poor husband and I are being taken disadvantage of by this fibber!"

The manager thought, trying to explain something to this bunch would be like trying to poke hot butter up a wildcat's ass in a closed cage. "Now listen, friends. This is what's going on, merely a little mistake in understanding, a mere figure of speech gone awry."

Legal Bagel took out his pad and put on his best lawyer's frown.

Mr. Daily Sufferer tried to explain further. "I said that I would give them an oil change in the morning."

Legal Bagel asked, "Then what's the problem?"

The manager answered, "They thought it was free."

Betty stomped her foot and said, "We asked you when you would be free to give us an oil change, and you said that you could give us an oil change in the morning."

"Yes! But I didn't mean for nothing."

"You did, you fibber, when you said it, you, you, something or another. I can't say it, but you should know what I mean to say and that makes you needing your mouth washed out with soap. So there!"

Legal Bagel yelled, "Order in the court! Sorry. I forgot where we were. Let's see where we are in this arbitration. I'll ask a few questions for clarification."

The manager thought, everything just went to hell.

" Felonious Perpetrator," Legal Bagel accused. "Sorry about that. I mean, manager. Did I hear you say 'free to give' or not?"

"Yes, but . . ., " stammered Mr. Sufferer.

"Just answer the question. We will explain your rights after we convict you of trying to cheat these poor people."

To help things at this tense moment a committee from the Blue-Haired Ladies Club called The Watch Cats, and I do mean cats, of the complex arrived to complain about the rain. They felt the management should exercise more control over such events as the weather. Twice this year their garden parties were interrupted by rain.

Ding-A-Ling was sneaking out of the office as the boss pleaded, "Help!"

And Ding-A-Ling said, "Boss, remember when I asked you for that extra day off three years ago to attend that girl's wedding who I hated?

"You said, no, that we were having our busiest and most difficult day, as if that was more important than a chance to pick at everything she wore."

"Get to the point, Ding-A-Ling. What are you trying to say?"

"To put it simply, boss, so I can make your day and get my revenge, there is also a delegation outside from the recently formed We Like Being Mooned Society. They are making demands for more frequent appearances of Miss Goodies and a schedule of the same, for their approval."

Legal Bagel said, "I represent that organization of complex thinkers and I will take up their plight next but right now we have heard the overwhelming evidence in our behalf. What do you have to say for your losing side, Mr. Suffering Manager? Before you speak, remember, I was head of the inquisition, oops, investigation department for HUD and I intend to apply the same fair and brutal tactics here."

"Don't say anything!" yelled Mr. Miser, one of the minor stockholders who just entered with his staff of lawyers.

Daily Sufferer knew that fink, Miser had his office bugged.

Mr. Miser said, "Well, Legal Bagel, we finally meet over a case of such magnitude that it warrants our respective skills. I've brought in my top man for this one. I'm sure you are familiar with Mr. Yellow Legal Pad."

"Yes. Didn't he make his name by losing an open and shut case to a first year law student?"

"That's why we are here, to settle this case out of sight."

"Okay with me. This is what my clients, the Scuppers want. For their pain and suffering for having to go through this ordeal, we want the bill torn up in small pieces. For their loss of prestige, defamation of their good name, and the time lost in their endeavor to do nothing, we want a simple apology from that sucker, of a manager, on his knees. Also, Betty gets to stomp her foot and say, 'So there!'"

Mr. Miser rising to the occasion, said, "We reject this proposal out-of-hand and this is our counter offer. Firstless, the bill will be torn in half. Secondless, the apology will be whispered and we will submit to either the 'so there' or the stomp, but not both."

"Impossible Miser, you offer us nothing. Put something on the table I can go to my people that has teeth in it."

Betty meekly said, "Mr. Bald Eagle, we think . . ."

Patting Betty's hand, Legal Bagel said, "I know, darling, you are suffering even more from their highhanded tactics, but we will endeavor to persecute."

"Okay, Bagel. This is our last offer. The bill will be torn into four parts. The apology will be mumbled in private and we will submit to a 'there' and a pat of her left foot. Take it or leave it."

After two serious seconds of thought, Bagel said, "We accept."

The manager, followed by the Scuppers walked into his office to apologize. After all, he needed his job. With one ex-wife and three kids, one present wife and two more kids, and a now pregnant girlfriend, these were real motivations for him to keep his job.

Before Mr. Sufferer could speak, Bilge said, "Sir, please don't apologize. Sometimes when people think they have a pain-in-the-ass situation, a lot of times they themselves are the pain in the ass. And, sir, we will pay the bill if it would help."

Betty cooed, "Oh, Bilge, that's so romantic."

"Mr. Scuppers and wife, I think you are the only people who would not take this chance to screw us over. So, I'm glad to give you this oil change."

The Scuppers waved goodbye to everybody in the office. As they left, few people paid them any mind. The Ownership and Legal Bagel were locked in a deep discussion trying to come up with the proper day for it to rain so they could placate the Blue-Haired Ladies Committee.

As they were walking back to the boat, Betty said, "Bilge, "I'm so proud of the way you kept them from taking disadvantage of us."

"I love the way you stood up for us too, honey. You know one of my famous sayings, 'Free is free and free is for me.'"

"Oh, Bilge, you are so smart and I'm glad you offered to pay the bill."

News travels fast around a marina and as usual gets screwed up in the telling. Everyone knows that dockmen don't tell tales, BUT when our two heroes returned, Princess was waiting.

"Betty, I heard about your terrible time in the office when you tried to insist on paying your bill. The nerve of them trying to charge you double and wanting you to apologize for offering cash."

And Betty said, "Welllll, it wasn't quite like that but . . ."

Bilge thought as he headed down below, bad enough I have to listen to my wife's gossip but I'm not going to stand here and listen to these two birds chirp. So there.

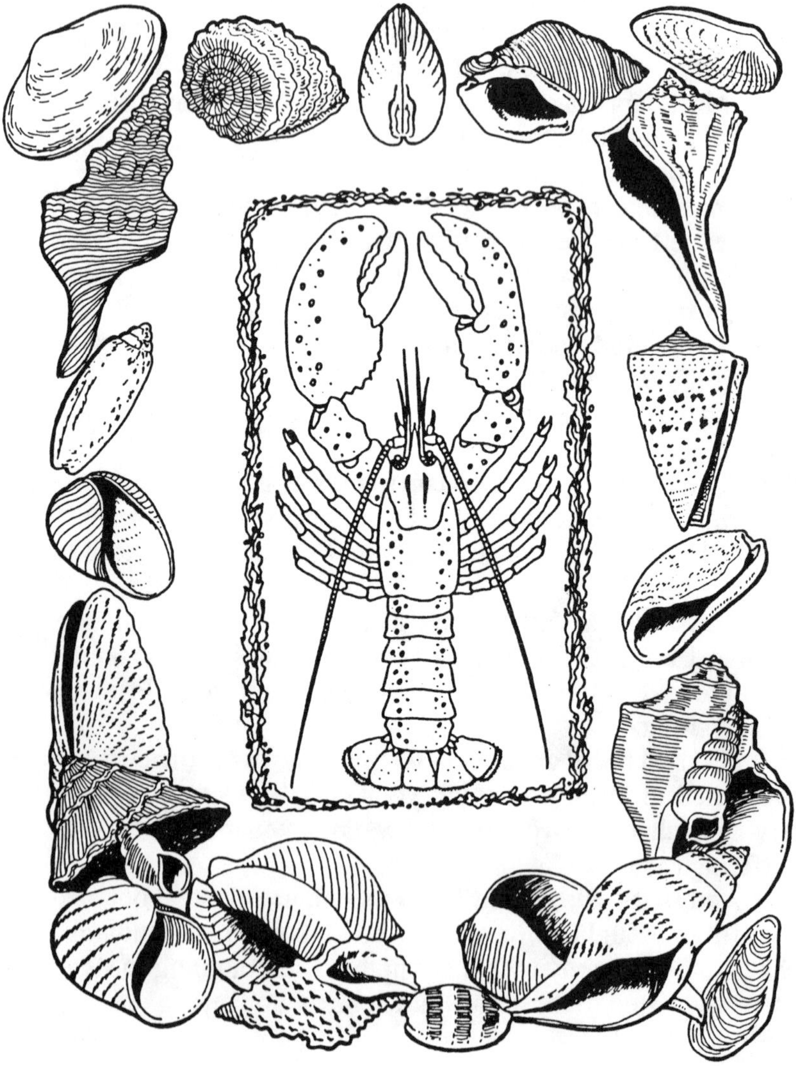

# CHAPTER THIRTEEN

Anyway, Bilge and Betty settled into their demanding schedule of boat life: up in the morning at eight, coffee and breakfast till ten. Then, Betty would start what she called her "mommy things" – cleaning the boat interior, washing clothes, and all that kind of good stuff.

Bilge would involve himself in very important activities like BS'ing with the neighbors. From time to time he would hose down the exterior of the boat, or fix things so well that they would have to be replaced. He felt the most important thing he could do was to give Betty advice.

One bright sunny morning when the weatherman predicted rain, Betty, after her nagging, convinced Bilge to give MY MISTAKE a sorely needed, first-class wash down. Betty had everything ready: buckets, wash cloths, brooms, brushes of various types, and an assortment of soaps and polish.

"Betty, what are we going to do with all that stuff? For crying out loud, we could wash the QUEEN MARY with that much junk."

Betty gave Bilge a couple of good eye squints and stated, "What does washing come under? Cleaning, that's what. And I'm in charge of cleaning. So there."

"Your cleaning domain does not cover the outside of the boat. So, I'm in charge."

"Who came up with that pooty poo? Cleaning is cleaning no matter where it is. Now, that's mine to boss."

"No way, Betty. You said the outside of the boat was mine to boss and I'm going to boss it."

"I distinctly said that the outside was for you to take care of like the inside was for me to take care of, but that does not have anything to do with cleaning. To take the cleaning-bossing away from a woman would be like separating church and state."

Bilge loved Betty too much to argue with her even if there was very little reasoning to her arguments. He loved Betty and he could never come up with a good reason why. His reply was, "I just love her too much to come up with a sensible reason."

That old sad-eyed, hang-dog look came over his face and he asked, "Little bride, are we having a fight?"

"Not if I win, poopsy baby. So I will apologize for your being a poot and I'll do anything I want. Now you see, Mommy settled the whole thing."

Bilge thought, I've been had again.

"Bilge, stop that thinking out loud and I will let you hold the hose and scrub all the hard places I can't reach. Now, how's that?"

Standing up for all macho husbands determined to get in the last word, Bilge said, "Yes, honey."

Bigshot overheard Bilge and said, "What the hell are we going to do with this guy?"

Princess said, "Leave him alone, that's what."

"Yes, honey."

---

Anyway, Bilge started spraying everything down and Betty began scrubbing the daylights out of the boat.

Just then a man came running down the quay in a panic. "Stop! Stop! For Godsakes, you are using the wrong soap, the wrong sponge, and your bucket doesn't even match your brush."

Bilge turned his head quickly to see who was threatening the safety of the boat. He twisted around to see who was running up the dock and, in doing so, he turned the hose slightly which placed it perfectly in line with Betty's behind. She received a long cold spray of water . . . @#$$%$@#$&*@#$#$%&*

"Sorry, Betty. No, honey, I didn't mean it. I promise, honey, I didn't mean it."

Bigshot yelled, "Save your breath, Bilge."

Ole Bilge had yet to learn that there are some things in life which threaten a man's existence like sticking your head in a loaded cannon, kicking a sleeping leopard, not paying your taxes or robbing Fort Knox. All of these sins can be forgiven, but spraying your wife's behind with cold water is not one of them.

Betty marched past Bilge on her way to change clothes. She smiled sweetly at Bilge for the benefit of the guests and whispered, "I HATE YOU!"

The Princess heard Betty's remark and immediately whispered to Bigshot, "I heard what she said."

[GOD FORBID, THIS NOSEY BROAD SHOULD MISS A THING!]

As Bilge was coming out of shock, he finally realized the thing he was squeezing was the trigger on the hose when he should have been squeezing this nut's neck. He was confronted with a flock of nosey neighbors.

And Princess said, "Good morning, Bilge. Is your wife angry at something?"

[SHE WAS PEEKING OUT OF THE WINDOW AND SAW THE WHOLE THING BUT HER TYPE ALWAYS HAS TO ASK, ANYWAY.]

Bilge answered, "Not really, Princess. She was just expressing her inner emotion in relation to a flow of cold water hitting her in the behind. Of course, some people always have cold behinds and would never know it happened."

Bigshot said, "You're showing some hidden hostility, Bilge, old buddy, that I didn't know you had."

Bilge said, "When it comes to Betty, old buddy, everybody better watch his step."

Betty emerged in time to say, "So there."

Princess said, "Oh, you know, Bilge darling. I didn't mean anything, just curious."

The tall thin fellow who did all the yelling looked like a mop himself. He said, "I'm so glad I stopped you before you embarrassed us or got yourself into trouble."

Bigboat Bigshot handled the introductions, "Bilge, this is Willow Wash-Down, and the sad little lady coming down the dock is his wife, Poor Pitiful Pearl."

Betty emerged dried out and still mad as hell. She gave Bilge a couple of eye squints to let him know he was still in some deep pooty poo. She said, "Hello, everybody. I'm glad to meet you."

The boys went into their huddle and the girls moved off into theirs.

Willow Wash-Down advised, "Bilge, I don't like to tell a man what to do, but [HERE IT COMES.] you almost made the tragic mistake of using the wrong soap on your boat. I used it for years until this new soap came out about a year ago and then I changed to a better one about three months ago. Then, this new one came out about two weeks ago. I understand they are coming out with a new one in a month, but I haven't tried it yet. You know what I mean? And another thing, everybody on this quay has brushes from Fuller Strings Brush Company."

Bigshot looked down his nose and said, "Bilge, I noticed your brush color doesn't match your bucket and your bucket clashes with your boat. We can't have that on Quay Zero, which IS the number one quay, now can we?"

Willow Wash-Down added, "My God, Bilge, that hose looks like it came from K-Mart or Sears where the working class shop."

Bigshot added, "Bilge, you're a lucky boy to have Willow Wash-Down on the same quay with you. He'll keep you up with the latest trends on soaps and buckets and protect you from the professional boat cleaners."

Bilge asked, "Tell me. Why am I lucky?"

"Why? Man, do you realize Willow Wash-Down holds the record for the most consecutive years for having washed his boat on Christmas? Why, not only does he wash his boat every day, he has the shiniest bright work in the marina. I have to admit, Mr. Total Teak spends most of his waking hours rubbing his decks, but he is not on the same quay so you see he loses a little class."

Bilge was thinking, I've spent my life in ladies' underwear and I've been BS'ed by experts. Now, I have to listen to these two amateurs tell me about products and trends. Who the hell cares if the hoses, buckets, and soaps don't match?

Bilge said, "Well, boys, I know a little bit about changes in products, that is. I've spent the last thirty years trying to fit half the women's backsides in New York, and one thing I've learned is that if it fits, you will wear it. If you buy something because someone gave you some advice, then you wind up with your drawers full of drawers that you don't wear. Now you expect me to tell Betty that she has all the wrong things to clean this boat with? The whole damn bunch of you are crazy. So there."

Anyway, on Betty's side of the world . . .

Princess said, "Betty, Poor Pitiful Pearl is so interesting to talk to. She has had so many operations that she will gladly tell you about and you'll hear about them at least three or four times. I just love the one about the cute OB-GYN with the cold hands and the one about the weird proctologist with the shakes."

Bilge glanced at Betty and gave her one of those "please forgive me, honey" smiles.

Betty gave him one in return that said, "you're forgiven but I won't let you live it down for a while, even after I buy myself a present. So there. And I still love you. So there."

After the departure of their neighbors, Betty asked, "Were they helpful, Bilge?"

"Their advice was worth just what I paid for it, honey. Nothing. What the hell is with these guys, anyway? Everybody in this place has to do what the other guy does. I wonder if they've ever been told that that junk belongs in high school. To think we need a matching boat and bucket! How childish can you get!"

Betty was staring at their bucket and their other equipment and said, "Of all the foolishness, matching your bucket to your mop! Junior high school stuff, if you ask me, sweetie."

"Yeah! Who cares if none of our stuff matches and looks all out of place?"

"You're right, Bilge. Do they think we are going to stop everything and run to the store and buy everything again? Poo on their trends."

Bilge looked around to see if anyone was watching and said, "Betty, we could leave now when nobody is looking and return the colors that don't match."

Betty hurriedly said, "Let's see, the mop matches the boat. So, let's go with the mop as a guide. Bilge, run down the quay and see if everybody has a white hose with a blue or green stripe. And don't forget to check and see if the bristles on their brushes are white or yellow."

Bilge took off like a shot, running up and down the quay and checking out the neighbor's gear.

[BY THE TIME BETTY GOT DRESSED, HE COULD HAVE RUN TO CHINA.]

"Betty, for holy poo poo in the park! What's taking you so long to get dressed? We're just going to Wal-Mart."

"Bilge, be careful. Just because you are the captain it doesn't mean you can curse like a sailor. And another thing, don't you dare let people know we shop any place other than those expensive boat stores where you have the privilege of paying twice as much for everything."

"Sorry, Betty, darling. For a moment I let my phony face slip."

Betty hid her embarrassing out-of-trend brush and bucket in a large bag and they hurried down the dock to the bus stop.

When our definitely in-trend boaters returned, it was to the smiles of approval from their considerate neighbors.

Once again Bilge and Betty started the task of washing down MY MISTAKE, secure in the idea that they would not embarrass anyone on Quay Zero.

A strange thing happened. Bilge returned to the strenuous task of hosing down and Betty returned to her God-given purpose of scrubbing everything in sight. No other husbands have had thoughts like Bilge as he was holding the new hose with Betty bent over in that same very interesting position with her cute butt up in the air and her sundress flying.

Betty warned without turning her head, "Don't even think about it."

And Bilge said what all guilty husbands would say, "Who, me? I wasn't thinking anything."

Bilge also knew that after a set number of years of marriage a wife becomes like a mother. They tune into your brain or develop eyes in the back of their heads. Maybe they plant little electrodes in your brain when you're sleeping or something. Whatever it is, Betty always seemed to know when he was about to do something naughty. Bilge felt that personally, this evil gift should have been cancelled when they moved on the boat.    But he's not saying a darn thing.

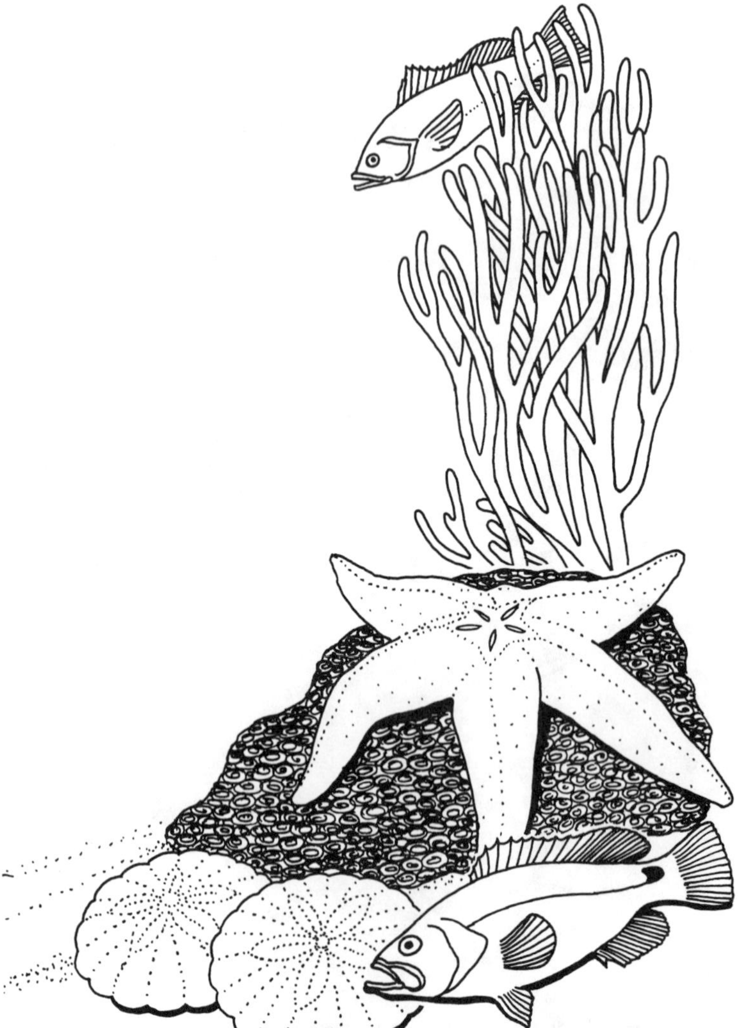

# CHAPTER FOURTEEN

Yelling, screaming, and with arms waving, Voom Voom ran down the quay in a panic and said, "The weatherman said there's a hurricane coming this way!"

Everybody came running out of his boat like a dumped over bee hive.

Bigshot asked, "Do you have any accurate coordinates on where it is located, Voom Voom?"

The Princess rushed over and said, "I just heard the weatherman say that it's absolutely maybe, coming here. It's an extreme, directly, unlikely possibility that we are definitely going to get it."

Bilge said, "That sounds serious to me."

Betty said, "We don't have hurricanes in New York. Why do they bother to have them down here? I'm sure the insurance company and us boaters could get along perfectly well without them. Anyway, what will happen to the poor dope people running around in those little boats I saw on 'Miami Vice'?"

Charlie Try-Em-All came out of his boat zipping up his pants, followed by Miss Goodies who was trying to fit ten pounds of boobs into a two-pound bra.

Charlie yelled, "Bilge, turn on your TV and let's get the latest."

The brave group crowded around the TV to hear Florida's Number One weatherman, according to him, that is. Somehow, every damn channel claims to have the number one weatherman.

"Weather watchers, this is your Number One weatherman, giving you the latest on Hurricane Schmuck. Remember, folks, we are the weather team who received the most awards for predicting the most accurate, maybe-it-will-rain forecast. Being right fifty percent of the time, we also were correct on our prediction that maybe-it-would-not-rain. Sooooooo, you know you are tuned into a team you can rely on. The rumor spread by the National Weather Service that I would be more reliable in my predictions if I climbed a goddamn tree to see what was coming is completely erroneous. The proof of that is, I get dizzy from heights.

"What? What? Pardon me, folks. My program director is trying to give me some late breaking news. What was that? Stop the crap and get on with the report? There must be something wrong with the cue cards.

"Now for my latest report. The killer hurricane which is nearing our coast is located two thousand miles out in the south Atlantic and is headed this way. I base my sound advice on the fact that all hurricanes head west. And after all, we are in the western hemisphere. Sooooo, I am predicting and remember, folks, you heard it here first, that this killer storm will come ashore somewhere between South America and the North Pole.

"To be precise in this forecast, I can confidently say that the killer storm called Schmuck is packing winds of an undetermined magnitude and traveling at various speeds. I advise everyone to stock up immediately. The storm should be here in two weeks. This is your Drippy Weather Show brought to you by Prophylactic Hardware and Raunchy's Grocery where you can get your hurricane supplies."

The group of TV watchers, after hearing such an informative weather report, looked at each other with a strange, what-did-that-idiot-say frown.

Bigshot, the in-command type, said, "Well, that's clear enough. I think we should all prepare immediately for the worst."

Betty was shaking her head and Bilge felt as if he wanted to hear more before he grabbed his boat and ran.

Willow Wash-Down came over and said, "I always watch the other guy, and the other guy, who has the famous program called 'The Other Guy's Number One Weather Program', said that the reports on the killer storm are coming in sketchy because the weather plane was blown up by the Jihad. They mistakenly thought that it was Air Force One." He added, "Anyway, the other guy claims he has a taller tree and is not afraid of heights."

Each person drifted off into his own confusion. The brave souls in Uppity A'ss Marina took their boats inland to specially rented slips for hurricane protection. It so happens that the marina makes a lot of money scaring the hell out of boat owners.

"Bilge, honey, should we be afraid?"

"Betty, this sounds to me more like a new line of underwear coming out instead of a storm. Everybody you listen to is trying to cover his ass with the latest report. We'll wait and see. If it gets close, honey, we can panic with the best of them. Anyway, storm reports are for the professionals who work to protect us and not the damn fools who get caught in them."

Betty was really shaking her head now. "I understand, baby boy. You always did know when it was best for us to stay uninformed."

Now Bilge was shaking his head. And he said to Betty, "Let's do our own thing."

After two frantic weeks with the weather reports coming in every five minutes and adding to the confusion, the Number One Number One weatherman was forced up the pine tree by his program director poking his ass with a shotgun demanding he see what was coming. At the top of the tree, he issued an heroic, life-saving report. "HEEEEELLLLLLLP!"

The population took this as an emergency proclamation that all of South Florida was about to be blown away. The populace was led in flight by the Other Number One Number One weatherman who was closely followed by the brave politicians, who nearly ran over the fearless city leaders. This group was followed by the other weatherman who was battling the sailboat population for the single exit out of town. Close on their heels came the screaming powerboat owners in their frantic flight to safety led by MY MISTAKE.

All the gentlemen at the National Weather Bureau appreciated the Number One weatherman's warning to the populace. Not because the storm was going to hit Florida. It actually sheared off missing the western hemisphere by five hundred miles and ravaged Bermuda with ten to fifteen mile-an-hour gentle southerly breezes. The weather bureau's gratitude stemmed from the fact that this was the first time they were able to drive leisurely down the freeway after work.

The network's major problem resulted from their storm

prediction. The problem arose when the program director at the Number One Number One Weather Program was charged by the Society for the Prevention of Cruelty to Animals because he attempted to shake some weird screaming creature from the top of a pine tree. And once down, he threatened to blow the screaming animal's ass off.

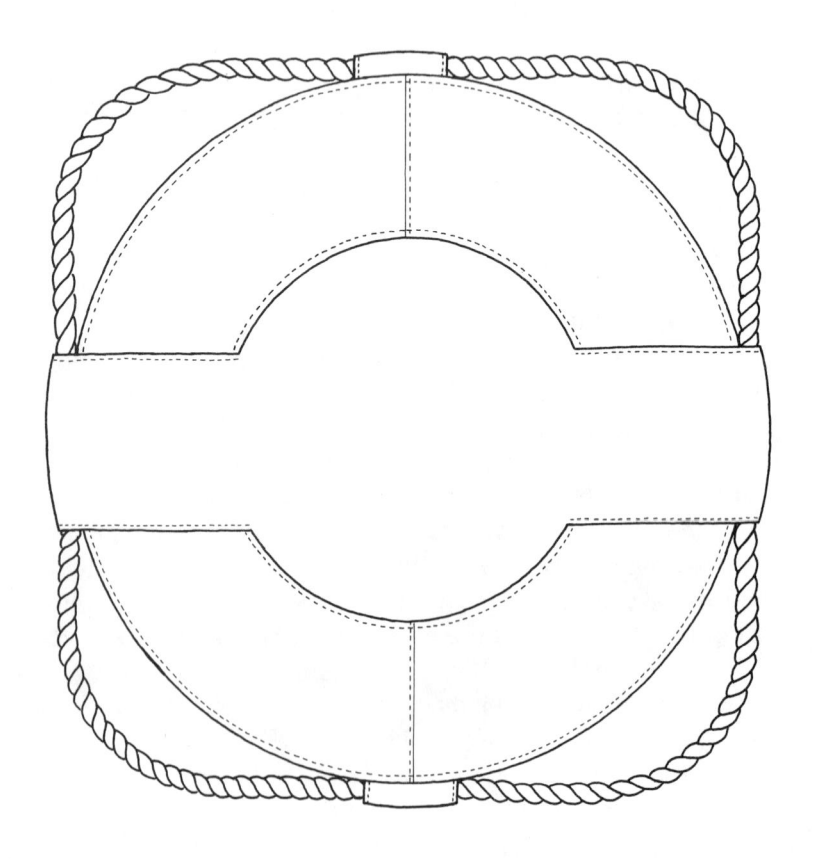

# CHAPTER FIFTEEN

The threat of the hurricane passed and the Scuppers returned from their frantic flight to safety, Bilge and Betty were having their favorite drink during sundowners that evening – two jiggers of gin, four ounces of cranberry juice, four ounces of grape juice, and two ounces of brandy – creating a drink named Bilg-A's. As ole Bilge says, "Anything over two of these and you can bet your ass you will be in the bilges."

"Bilge, honey, did you read what that poster said about the Keys?"

"Keys to what?"

"Not keys, silly, the Florida Keys."

"Oh, those Keys. Yeah, sweetie. I read it when I went to the pot."

"Bilge, don't you dare get descriptive. Remember, you're not that foul-mouthed writer. Anyway, what did you think about them?"

"Them what?"

"The Florida Keys, you silly goose."

"Well, I think we're almost ready to go on a great adventure to far distant lands, battling the elements, seeing strange creatures, meeting primitives, fighting . . ."

"Bilge, control yourself. We are only talking about South Florida."

"Sorry about that, Betty. I was just going by what the poster said."

"Bilge, honey, do we have enough fuel to get there?"

"I should think so, babe. Why?"

Whenever Betty heard Bilge say, "I think so", it was time to check it and damn quick. Betty was out of her chair and on the flying bridge like a shot and down again like a yoyo.

"Honey, both needles are on E. Does that mean 'enough' or 'empty' on a boat? Or, is there a third answer?"

"I'm pretty sure it means 'empty', honey. Why don't we take on fuel tomorrow? It will be thrilling."

"Oh, my goodness, Bilge, that means we'll have to move

the boat. What fun!"

"Mate, we'll get to use our free fuel tickets."

"Are you sure, captain? I think they meant it for the car that we don't own. Remember that man from Pollution Oil who came around taking the survey to find out who owned a car and who didn't? He wanted to make sure it was an honest contest and by chance, all those who didn't own a car won first, second, and third prize."

It was Bilge's turn to be on the run. He was back in a flash with the tickets. "Look here, it says fuel for one year, and it doesn't say cars or gas, or give any stipulations, except that you must be alive to win."

---

The next morning all of MY MISTAKE's lines were cast off. Some were on the dock, two stern lines were wrapped around the starboard piling, and one bow line was dangling in the water. Betty turned the bow line loose at the last moment or she would have wound up in the water with the lines. Bilge backed out and forgot she was hanging onto the line. Like a good old diehard woman, Betty held on to the bow line until the whole thing played out into the water.

After four tries, Bilge and Betty got within ten feet of the fuel dock, resulting in the dockmaster lassoing the quarter bit and they hauled MY MISTAKE to the dock.

The dockmaster said, "Good morning, Mr. and Mrs. Scuppers. That was an interesting landing. Mr. Scuppers, could I be so bold as to suggest that just one of you handle the controls at a time."

And Betty said, "Certainly not, you may not be bold or any other kind of person. The man at the Coast Guard said we are supposed to help each other when we are handling the boat in close quarters."

"Mrs. Scuppers, are you sure that's what the instructor meant when he said, 'to handle the boat together'?"

"I was there. Were you, Mr. Smarty Dock-Full-of-Advice?" Betty was still mad as hell at him for telling her to make it fast with the lines when they had first arrived at the marina.

"No, ma'am, I was not."

"Then, please don't contradict my notes. Unless you were aware of what was going on during those classes and the type of diligent future boaters who were asking inspirational questions, you had better not venture to comment."

The dockmaster rolled his eyes in surrender and asked, "Captain Scuppers, are you ready to take on fuel?"

If you ever want to get Bilge on your side, call him 'captain'.

In a very aloof captain's manner, Bilge said, "Why yes, Dockmaster, we are."

"Captain Scuppers, are your fuel tanks open and where are they located?"

Bilge looked to Betty for help and she looked to him for the same. [IN THIS CASE BOTH BLACKBOARDS WERE EMPTY.]

Betty said meekly, "Mr. Masterdocks, we don't know where they are. That Diggity Dog writer should have told us where they were instead of letting us get embarrassed by having to ask."

[VENGEANCE IS SWEET, SAYETH THE WRITER.]

The dockmaster said, "Permission to come aboard, Captain, and I'll help you find them."

Bilge said in his debonair captain's voice, "Permission transmitted."

After a quick search of the decks they found the port and starboard fill caps. The dockmaster explained to Bilge and Betty the technique of taking on fuel. Betty wrapped the end of the marina's fuel nozzle with paper towels, wiped off the fueling nozzle for the first time in its history, and then, allowed it to come aboard.

The dockmaster asked, "How much fuel do you intend to take on, sir?"

"Mr. Masterdock, it's another one of those things we weren't told."

"Bilge said, "Let's fill her up and find out."

They began to take on fuel. Betty was upset and kept

peering over the side to check the overflow after taking on 20 gallons of fuel. As the fuel meter continued to roll over and they passed 100 gallons in the starboard tank, both of the sweethearts nearly panicked.

"Bilge, where do you think it's all going?"

"I hope it's in the tanks, Betty. I'm getting worried." Bilge added, "Hold the handle, Betty. I'll go check, maybe it's going into the bilges."

Bilge was below and back like a yoyo. He said, "Betty, I don't see anything, I don't smell anything and I don't hear anything."

"Bilge, you sound like those monkeys on Mr. Chick-In-Sheet's desk. Ask Mr. Masterdock. Maybe, he knows what's happening."

At 225 gallons the starboard tank overflow started squirting into the water. The fuel dock attendant who was busy BS'ing on one of the other boats came running over saying, "Ya'lls is full on this side."

Betty said, "You mean we can put more in on the other side?"

"Yes ma'am, ya'lls can."

Betty said, "Bilge, I wonder where the tanks are?"

"I don't know, Betty. When the dockmaster comes back, we'll ask him to find them." After completing their fueling, the dockmaster returned with their bill. Bilge presented him with one of Pollution Oil's free fuel voucher slips.

After a close examination and a half a dozen phone calls to the marina office, the dockmaster said, "I guess this is okay. Anyway, I passed the responsibility off on somebody else."

Betty cooed, "Mr. Dockiemaster, you've been sooooo sweeeet. Do you mind telling us where you think the fuel tanks are? After all, we took on 550 gallons and we don't see any in the bilges or any place else."

"No trouble at all, ma'am. On the vessel of your type, a double cabin cruiser, they're under the beds in the master stateroom."

Betty gasped, "Ooooooohhh, my Gooodddddd! And I sleep on them! What if they go 'boom'? Bilge, I want them moved today. I mean right now. I refuse to sleep on fuel tanks."

"Betty, we can't move them, that's how the boat is built. They're built in, darling."

Betty ordered, "Then, build them out."

The dockmaster added, "Ma'am, that's how most yachts are built."

"Absolutely ridiculous! This is another one of those things where a woman was not consulted first."

---

Our two sailors cast off their lines. As the boat drifted away from the dock, they both dashed madly for the flying bridge to take over their assigned controls. After two circles and three attempts to back into their slip on this clear windless day, Betty dashed down and caught the lines from the dock attendants. One dockman was sitting in a boat with the bow line in hand but Betty refused to catch it because it was wet. She made him hang it on a piling until it was dry and got him a new one. No one dared to tell her to make it fast.

Betty received good seamanship comments like, "Ma'am, would you please place the eye on the bit?"

And a quick, "Ma'am, we'll come aboard and finish tying up."

Betty allowed the dock attendants to come aboard and complete the securing of MY MISTAKE but not before she inspected their shoes and hands.

Content that their major task of taking on fuel was completed, the couple spent the next three days in a soft relaxed atmosphere aboard their boat. Betty still did not like the idea of sleeping on fuel tanks and refused to let Bilge come anywhere near her. She refused to take a chance on all the rocking and shaking that would be going on in the bedroom. But love or horniness will win out in the end between two people who care about each other.

"Men are disgusting, especially romantic husbands and dirty thinking writers who tell on us. So there."

The Scuppers' voucher arrived at Pollution Oil's headquarters and disrupted many of the company's future plans. Mr. Prize-Butt, who conducts these contests had assured the board of directors that the contest would be conducted in a fair and unbiased manner. He knew exactly who would win and was sure that it would cost their company nothing. On the arrival of the voucher, many pointed and polite questions were asked of him.

"Who in the hell won this contest, Prize-Butt? They must own a damn truck line to use this much fuel at one time."

"What the F#$%@ happened, Prize-Butt? You said only people without cars would win fairly."

Pollution Oil is one of these companies, when you owe them money, they act on it instantly. They send their bills out immediately and demand their money consistently. Hence, the reason why the free voucher caused such turmoil.

A polite request was made of the contest manager. "Get your ass down there and find out what's going on. If you didn't plan this crooked contest fairly and if you can't straighten it out, when you get to the end of Florida, start swimming."

Mr. Prize-Butt, after meeting with the Scuppers, was last seen doing the backstroke past Cuba with various accumulated, types of sharks planning their menu.

It was decided by Pollution Oil, being a fair-minded bunch of world-polluting finks, that it would be necessary to get to the bottom of this contest problem. Realizing that honesty could get out of hand, they called in the FBI.

The FBI sent their top agent in the area to investigate if there was any wrongdoing, or any violations of interstate commerce, or any other laws that menace simple people who think they have won an honest contest.

Lo and behold, the top agent in the area happened to be a boat owner, who woke up one morning with a big sticky blob of black scum wrapped around his brand new sailboat. Agent Super-Snoop had written a polite letter requesting Pollution Oil, cease dumping sludge in the waterway. He received a polite "go screw yourself" letter in return.

The depth of his investigation of the Scuppers case consisted of... "Hello, Mr. and Mrs. Scuppers, I'm with the local FBI. I came here to make sure you won your contest fair and square. Sir, what I consider fair and square for Pollution Oil, is, for everyone to rob those dirty finks the first chance they get."

Before Bilge could answer the gentleman, the agent added, "Thank you, Mr. and Mrs. Scuppers, for helping me with my in-depth investigation. There will be no more questions, sir. And I can assure you that the full force of our agency will be behind you or the president will kick our ass. Sooooooooooooo, from my wife, Anti-Oil, and I... Officially there."

When Agent Super-Snoop returned to the office, his boss who had lost all his orange trees to a refinery expansion by Pollution Oil said, "We must investigate this case to its limits. Who in the hell is Pollution Oil and who are their principal stockholders? And who are these people who are mistaken about MY MISTAKE and caused the whole thing to be one big mistake?"

It turns out that everyone was mistaken about who owned Pollution Oil who was making all the mistakes of spilling all the oil into the waterways. The real owners, without a mistake, turned out to be Yo Shitty Mo Autos and I. Happily Fung U.S., Electronics of Japan. This news was leaked to the newspapers by a direct call from the FBI. At the same time a local newspaper made a threat to expose the sham that the Japanese owned half of Los Angeles. This sham was to divert the American people's attention away from the fact that they really owned all of Coral Gables, Florida, half of Palm Beach County, and three-fourths of Broward County.

The threats to expose Yo Shitty Mo Autos and I. Happily Fung U.S. Electronics as being the earth's raping, world-polluting giants they were, caused the conglomerate to graciously consider a settlement. After firing all the Americans above floor sweeper and importing their own homegrown finks, they extended Bilge and Betty's free fuel coupons for five years, only if they signed a waiver stating that they were responsible for the original mistake and that there would be no future mistakes by the owners of MY MISTAKE who initiated the whole mistake.

Along with Bilge and Betty's acceptance of these vague terms, Yo Shitty Mo Autos received in the mail on the same day an answer to their tuff shitty mo letter from General Conglomerate Motors. Bilge and Betty received a duplicate copy of these dubious dealings.

---

"Betty, what are you reading and squinting your eyes about?"

"Bilge, I'm trying to figure out what they mean in this letter. It's about us. You know how I hate it when I'm talking about people and they're so rude wanting to know what I'm saying about them. I can't stand people when they're that nosey and can't understand that you're talking about them and not to them."

Exasperated, Bilge asked, "Betty, what's in the letter?"

"Oh, that. It says here, addressed to us, but not to us.

'Dear Yo Shitty Mo Autos and your unmarried parent's company, I Happily Fung U.S., Electronics: After deep consideration and a long extended meeting by our executive board which took two minutes to act upon your complaint concerning the motor yot (yacht), MY MISTAKE'.

"What complaint, Bilge? We didn't complain to anyone."

"I don't know, Betty. What are they complaining about?"

"One company wants the other company to turn its name backwards and it says here. 'We came to a unanimous consensus of a parcel we don't give a shit, that you should reverse the name of your company to better suit the identity of your company. This would clarify your problem with the American vessel called MY MISTAKE.'

"Bilge, they're talking about our dear little boat in this letter and General Conglomerate Motors, says we were anchored legally in the fairway that is designated for our type of boat. It goes on to say, 'We at G C M bring to your attention that your vessel encroached upon the legal anchorage of MY MISTAKE which was participating in safe boating exercises in the ship channel with the Coast Guard.'

"You're right, Bilge. It was the ship's fault, aaaannnnnd G C M goes on to say that the Japanese ship's captain caused panic throughout South Florida with his threats to our little boat. 'General Conglomerate Motors wants it understood that they don't mean to over exaggerate.'

"Don't you think that's nice of them, Bilge? Aaaannnnd they further state: 'G C M hereby accuses Yo Shitty Mo Autos of causing the enormous expense of calling up the Naval Reserve, the Coast Guard, and various other organizations to protect American lives and property including that innocent little yot (yacht) from your illegal attempt to run over that vessel and encroach upon American rights.' Bilge, did you see any of that?"

"It must have happened right after we left, honey. You know our side would never exaggerate our problems."

"It also says here, Bilge, 'G C M wants you to understand from this letter we are firmly on the side of Yo Shitty Mo Autos.'"

"Betty, let me see that letter. Okay, it says here,

'So G C M recommends to you, Yo Shitty Mo Autos, to enable the American public to properly identify your company, we would like you to change your name to Happily We Fung U Yo Shitty Mo Autos.

Our warmest personal regards from all of us who don't really give a shit at G C M F.U., So Sorry . . .

P.S. Please direct your tuff shitty mo letters to the other four of the big five auto makers. Based on Japan's previous fair trade policy, they will help you kiss your trade problems goodbye by quickly turning a sympathetic REAR to all your problems.

Signed, All of us who wish to return to the gunboat policy of fair trade.'

"Betty, I totally agree with what I think I just read. What

do you think, honey?"

Betty was nodding her head. [YOU KNOW WHAT THAT MEANS.]

---

Anyway, a few days later an ultra secret meeting was held by the big shots of the major auto makers. A joint policy was agreed upon to make a financial settlement with the Scuppers and the price was fixed to the deal with them.

Betty had just returned to check her junk mail. Like wrong numbers, Betty loved to get junk mail and answer the letters as soon as possible.

"That's the only polite thing to do, Bilge, regardless of how silly they are. Look at this! We received a letter from the big five auto makers with checks in them."

"What the hell for, Betty?"

"Welllll, each one says the same thing.

'Dear Bilge and Betty Scuppers:

Thank you for your courageous stand against the unfair trade practice of Yo Shitty Mo Autos. Your fierce and daring stand in determined protest by your little boat blocking the channel and challenging a super ship of a foreign flag will always stand as a monument to our American way of life – apple pie, Mom, and all that good stuff to brave people like you.

P.S. We are enclosing a rebate check for one thousand dollars on the car you didn't buy.

From all of us: WHO DO GIVE A SHIT, THANKS BILGE AND BETTY'

"Bilge, did we do something I don't know about?"

"I think it's about the little ruckus we had with that Japanese ship, honey. A lot of people are like me. And you know what I always say, 'If it's not American, it's not.' But let's be nice and take their money. After all, the auto makers would gladly and politely take ours."

# CHAPTER SIXTEEN

Bilge and Betty returned to their marina way of life. Mornings at coffee and talking over good old times and good new times as Betty called them. Lunch was light, fruit or yogurt. Betty finally got Bilge to eat like a person instead of a salesman.

Evenings on the bow were their favorite time. Betty made popcorn in the microwave for their "or'derbies". That was Bilge's special name for their little treat with beer.

Betty was the quiet one this special evening.

Bilge asked, "Why so quiet, sweetie pie?"

"Oh nothing special, baby boy. It's just, Bilge, is there something called being too happy?"

"Well, prettiest girl in the world, I'm sure glad it's happening to us. You know what I was thinking? I was thinking I never have a chance to see you."

"That's silly, you goose. I'm with you everyday."

"Betty, wife, honey, and one sweet swinging girlfriend, I mean you. Not just your looks like, but you, babe. We were caught up in everything: work, friends, family, and all kinds of good stuff. Them times I didn't look close. Figured I had it made. You know what I'm trying to say. I had you, the job, two TV sets, you could watch your stuff and me mine. I saw my life with you and I loved it and you. But, sweet baby, I've had time since we've been on the boat, to see you and what you are, Betty person. And I like you, Betty person. Can we eat now? I'd like to watch TV early tonight."

"Bilge, you're so romantic. Sometimes, I don't know, I, I. . ." sniffle, sniffle.

"One thing I know, Miami better snap out of their crap or I'm going back to root for my old Giants."

"Bilge, are you sure you love me?"

"Sure I love you. Are we going to have chicken salad tonight?"

The sun was going down behind the lingering rain clouds that hung over the land, putting on a display of nature seen only on the water. The reds and yellows like a Van Gogh painting danced on the edges of clouds which were spread on the canvas of the sea, creating ever changing beauty.

"If chicken salad will make my baby boy happy that's what it will be."

"Great. I won't miss any of the game."

As they walked towards the stern, Bilge said, "Hey, Betty, you see that beautiful sunset? I like to feel as if I gave it to you as an, 'I love you' present."

"You just did, husband and lover. You just did."

---

Bilge chatted all through supper about what Miami should do to win the game. Betty knew little about football but it gave her a chance to remain in a quiet mood. And it made Bilge happy to have a listener.

After supper she finished her chores and returned to the main salon. She stood still watching her man raising hell at one team and then the other. She smiled, then wiped the tears from her eyes, and walked to the bow. She stood quietly looking out over the water and watched the twinkling of faraway lights.

Her mood deepened and she expressed her thoughts aloud. "I know I'm a good person, and Bilge loves me for that. I've become a real person and not just a wife and now I do my own talking. I really met my guy on this boat and I've been his girlfriend, wife, and mommy ever since. Now that I said that, God, can I talk to you now? I don't expect you to answer me, especially me being some character in a crazy book. I'm made up of all of us ladies who follow their husbands aboard boats, so that makes me somebody, I hope. But if you will just listen, it would be nice. I'm sorry I didn't spend a lot of time with you except on holidays, weddings and funerals. But Bilge told me that he believed God was God and that was enough for him and it's enough for me. As simple as that statement is and as unsimple as it is, I think that what I say next is the same. Not as big as you, Lord, of course, but here it is. I love my guy and I thank you, God, that I have him. He's a boater and we need you, us boaters that is, need I say more?"

Betty started to return to the main salon to hug her man and thought she heard a voice say, "I LIKE YOU, BETTY PERSON."

[FORGIVE THIS TEAR FROM A GROUCHY OLD WRITER, BUT BILGE AND BETTY ARE REAL TO ME AS ALL THE WONDERFUL PEOPLE WHO LOVE THEIR BOATS AND HAVE FOUND EACH OTHER.]

---

Anyway, the next morning Bilge informed Betty that they were going to the club for a quiet evening of dancing.

"Just you and me, babe. No neighbors. We can cut a fancy rug to the music all by ourselves."

"Bilge, I don't have anything to wear."

"Betty, for Pete's sake. You have a whole locker full of clothes."

"Men don't understand anything. Just because I have a locker full of clothes doesn't mean I have anything to wear."

Bilge spent the day polishing the hell out of everything on the boat. He had caught two common, contagious boat diseases going around marinas. "Your boat is not going to shine better than mine", and "My teak is going to look better than yours even if it kills me."

On the other hand, Betty busied herself around the galley to keep from going crazy over what to wear. After trying on three or four different outfits, she confronted Bilge for help.

"Bilge, what do you think of this one?"

"I like it, honey."

"What do you like about it?"

"It looks nice."

"How nice?"

"Real nice."

"Not that kind of nice. What kind of nice?"

"I don't know. It just looks nice on you."

"I knew all along you didn't like this one. Neither do I."

Betty was down and back in a flash.

"What about this one?"

"That one looks great on you, too."

"Greater than the other one?"

"Just as great, honey, and maybe a little greater."

"God, Bilge, can't you see this one makes me look fat?"

[THE POOR MAN MADE THE MISTAKE OF AGREEING WITH A LADY WHEN SHE WANTS YOU TO DISAGREE.]

"Why yes, honey. Now that you mention it, it does seem to put a little weight on you."

Tears began to flow. Betty stomped her foot and said, "I hate everything and especially you, for calling me fat."

Bilge gave up and headed out on deck. When it was time to go she emerged all smiles wearing a white jumpsuit with the silver earrings and silver pearls that Bilge had given her many years ago.

"Wellll, what do you think?"

"Betty, you're so gorgeous I'm afraid to let anybody see you but me."

[TALK ABOUT A GUY GETTING HIMSELF OFF OF BETTY'S POOT LIST.]

"Betty, I don't remember you buying that outfit. When did you get it?"

"You silly goose, I bought this two years ago and I just hated it. Men don't remember anything important."

"Why are you wearing it, if you hate it?"

"For goodness sake, Bilge. I don't hate it now. I love it."

[BILGE WALKED AWAY LIKE ALL GOOD HUSBANDS SHOULD AT A TIME LIKE THIS.]

Bilge was in a gay mood tonight. Betty had served a little toddy while they were dressing.

"Betty, what should I wear tonight?"

"I have it all laid out for you, husband. You are wearing your dark gray blazer, white pants, white shirt, and your black Ascot."

[BILGE LOOKED LIKE A WELL-DRESSED, BLACK-THROATED SEA GULL.]

Upon arriving at the club, Bilge asked if his table was ready.

Pansy Tight-Ass, the head waiter, cooed, "Ooooohh, yessss. You're the Scuppers who promised the big tip if I found you a quiet table. I have just the thing for you, Captain Scuppers . . . nice and quiet, next to the dance floor."

Bilge asked, "Do you think the band will disturb us?"

Tight-Ass said, "Sir, the average age of the band is the same as the Apostles. If Ruddy Toot Toot and his Three Gazoots play loud enough for everyone to hear, half the members will have to jump start their pacemakers and the other half with hearing aids will blow a fuse. I'm sure you will be pleased with your table. Please follow me."

Tight-Ass had a wiggle that Marilyn Monroe would envy as he led Bilge and Betty to their table.

"Oh Bilge, look at the flowers! Who ordered them, as if I didn't know who ordered them?" Betty picked up the card and squinted her eyes to read Bilge's love note. "To you know who from you know who and you know why."

Betty let out a quiet, "Meeeeeoooowwww, you're soooooo romantic, I'm so happy I'm going to cry all night when I get home."

Ruddy Toot Toot led or coaxed his band into one of the oldies but no goodies and Bilge asked, "Hey, cutie, how about cutting the rug with me?"

Betty, with eyelashes flashing and being as coy as she could, said, "I seldom dance with strangers unless they ask me, handsome."

Bilge and Betty had taken two complete courses in dancing at the YMCA. Betty was full of natural rhythm but could never remember the steps. Bilge, on the other hand, couldn't carry a tune in a bucket, but was able to learn the steps.

With his stooped shoulders, Bilge held Betty close to him which gave the appearance that he had a backbreaking hold on her. They moved around the floor with a stiff grace.

Bilge followed the set routine taught in the classes. He followed one beat, his own. Jerry Lee Lewis could be knocking himself out and Bilge would still be at the old two-step pace.

After that dance and a polite little applause, Bilge and Betty returned to their table to be greeted by Bigshot and Princess. They were sitting at the next table with their guests, Voom Voom and Straightlace.

Bigshot said, "You two cut a handsome couple, Bilge. We didn't know you were coming over tonight. Why didn't you tell us?"

From the tone of Bigshot's voice, Bilge got the impression that he needed this jerk's permission. "Well, Bigshot, this is a very special evening for Betty and me. And I just thought we'd do this one by ourselves."

[THERE'S ONE THING YOU'LL NEVER GET BY WITH THE PRINCESS AROUND, THAT'S THE LACK OF A DETAILED EXPLANATION SO SHE CAN TWIST IT AROUND IN HER OWN IMAGINATION.]

"What is this special evening?" Princess asked.

Bilge said, "Betty is my special evening."

Bigshot said, "Bilge, you better stop that kind of talk. Everybody's going to think you're in love with your wife. Do you realize, fella, you could give marriage a bad name like that?"

Betty was thinking bad thoughts but she was too much of a lady to say them. And from the looks that passed between Princess and Straightlace, she wasn't the only one.

Voom Voom said, "Oh God, guess 'what' just arrived?"

Princess demanded, "Who? Who? Who? Tell me."

Voom Voom said, "Don't look or stare at him, you'll make his night, but it's that premier asshole, Horny Riggings."

Bigshot with his loud, show-off manners, yelled across the dance floor, "Hey, Horny, come over here. I want you to meet some friends of mine."

Horny came to the table and stood very close to Straightlace, who froze like a statue of a nun. Horny was one of those men who could never stand still when he was around women. Bilge noticed as he walked across the dance floor that half the women headed for the pee parlor to make sure he wasn't going to ask them to dance.

Bigshot said, "Horny, ole buddy, these are my new friends. And as friends of mine, you know they are top drawer. This is Bilge and Betty Scuppers."

Bilge stood to shake hands with Horny Riggings, but if he was there ole Horny didn't acknowledge him. He was too busy massaging Betty's hand all the way up to her elbow. Betty got the feeling that any moment this guy was going to break into the mating dance of a prairie chicken.

Horny asked Bilge as he dragged Betty towards the dance floor, "You don't mind if I dance with your wife, do you? Thanks."

What does a sweet little wife do when placed in an embarrassing position by an embarrassing jerk? She does what Betty did. She made the best of the situation.

Bilge took a quick look at Bigshot sitting there grinning about his success in upgrading the Scuppers. Bilge remembered an old cliché, "If I could buy this jerk for what he's worth and sell him for what he thinks he's worth, I'd have enough money to hire Trump as a houseboy."

When Bilge and Betty danced, she danced as far forward as possible to be close to his stoop-shouldered stance. It was just the opposite with Horny. If he would have gotten any closer to Betty he would have been standing in back of her. She struggled through the dance and as soon as the music ended, she pulled free from his clutching hands and headed for the ladies' room.

Horny returned to the table wearing the smile of a successful rapist and said, "I just can't wait to have another dance with that little gal."

Bilge said, "You know, Horny, we're in polite company so I'm going to say this as politely as I can under these circumstances. The next dance you have with one of us Scuppers is going to be with me out in the parking lot, you son-of-a-b@#$%%$@*. Now, sir, was I too subtle or would you like to start the dance here?"

Horny, like his type at all the clubs, said what they always say. "Too bad, Bigshot. I thought your friend was one of us and could handle a little friendly play."

Bilge was never a man to anger easily unless it came to the one thing in life that meant more to him than anything, Betty's happiness.

Horny looked down his nose at Bilge as if there was dog poo on Bilge's shoes and walked away.

Bigshot said, "Bilge, you embarrassed one of my best friends."

Bilge said, "Sorry, Bigshot, but I enjoyed it."

Betty returned with eyes a little red and her head tilted down in embarrassment.

Princess said, "Betty and Bilge, Horny doesn't mean anything by the way he acts. Everybody accepts him because he always acts that way. But when he gets down to it and it's time to go for it, he's as frightened as a little boy."

She added quickly as she gave a terrifying look towards Bigshot, "That's what I was told by one of the single girls here. I don't know for sure myself and it would not be anything I would know first hand and it's definitely something I never was involved in."

If one could read the minds of all those present, except for her jerk husband who thought he was so magnificent, his wife would never look at any other man, one would hear the lines spoken loud and clear by Lawrence Olivier, "I DARE SAY, YOU PROTEST YOUR INNOCENCE TOO MUCH."

Bilge said, "Well, I got a feeling he's going to take his act to somebody else's stage. Are you okay, Betty?"

"Dance with me, Bilge, and hold me for a little while." Our two simple unsophisticated, un-modern and out-of-the-times sweethearts danced to "Me And My Shadow" and held each other closely. Nothing more needs to be said... not when it's real between two people.

When they returned to their table, Betty dried her tears and the evening began again.

Commodore Pompous-Ass arrived with his entourage. To his chagrin, the band didn't play a salute and no one knelt.

"Good evening, my friends. I'm sure one of you lovely people would love to buy me a drink. Wouldn't you, Bigshot?"

With that he plunked his unwelcome pompous ass in between Bigshot and Bilge.

Pompous-Ass said, "Bilge, my son, the waiter said that you and your bride are having a quiet evening together. How nice."

"Yeah, I had a quiet evening just like this at a Mets game."

"Funny, funny, Bilge. By the way, have you seen my pictures of the trip to the Keys? You must, Bilge. It's the place to go. Take my word for it."

Bilge asked, "Have you sailed there, Commodore?"

"Of course not. I have pictures from someone else's trip and that's just as good."

"Bilge?"

"Yeah, Betty?"

"Pay me some mind."

"Sorry, honey. I meant to tell you why we came tonight, but I haven't had a chance."

"Tell me now."

"I wanted it to be special, Betty."

"Now," she demanded.

Bilge reached into his pocket and brought out a little box and handed it to Betty.

"What is it?"

"Open the box."

Betty opened the box and read the card. It said, "Happy birthday to the sweetest lady who is still a little girl playing ladies on one of those big zeroes that are so painful. I hope you will forgive me for reminding you of your birthday."

Betty started to sniffle and said, "I tried to let it slip by without you thinking I was not a little girl anymore." Betty removed two gold anchor earrings from the box and after a quick, "Oh, Bilge, you shouldn't have," she took off like a shot to the ladies' room to put them on.

Princess followed and said while looking down her jealous nose, "They are small, but cute. What are they for?"

"My birthday."

Princess said, "My husband bought me the same kind, much bigger of course, but not for my birthday."

Betty had her limits, too, and asked, "What were they for,

Princess, to shut you up?"

Anyway, after a boring evening listening to the same old boring crap from their neighbors, our two sailors walked back to their boat singing songs, hugging each other, and planning their tomorrows.

"Bilge, let's have one more drinky poo on the bow before we go to bed."

"You're on, cute stuff. Two drinky poos coming up. They should turn on your sexy button."

"Bilge, watch your naughty talk even if I like it sometimes ... like now."

They sat quietly on the bow on this quiet evening with the moon on the water, the sounds of distant music drifting over the waves, a soft drone of a far off motor, a night bird calling, a splashing noise from the desperate leap of a fish trying to survive one more night and the ding of a church bell's late chime. The red and green lights of the harbor entrance beckoned a late arrival to safety. The late arrival entered, backed into its slip, turned off its engines, then all that power was quiet as the two sweethearts became overwhelmed by it all. No words came for a while. None were needed.

Then ...

"Bilge, let's go to the Keys after the small boat handling class."

"You know what I was thinking, Betty? I was thinking we should go to the Keys, too."

"Honey, that is the last class we have to take and I know you'll understand at least half of what is going on and I'll understand the other half, so we should be okay."

"Yeah, Bilge, us two halves make a good whole on the water."

## Crossing Situations

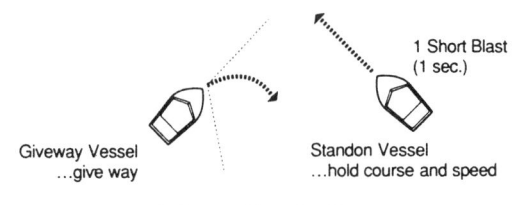

Giveway Vessel
...give way

1 Short Blast (1 sec.)

Standon Vessel
...hold course and speed

## Meeting Head-On or Nearly So

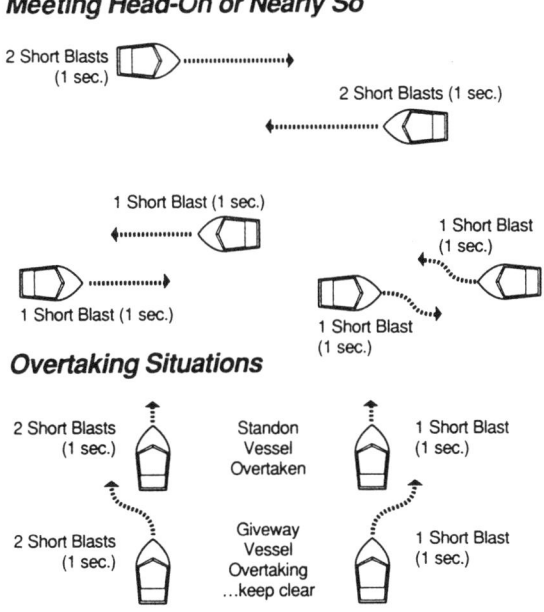

2 Short Blasts (1 sec.)

2 Short Blasts (1 sec.)

1 Short Blast (1 sec.)

1 Short Blast (1 sec.)

1 Short Blast (1 sec.)

1 Short Blast (1 sec.)

## Overtaking Situations

2 Short Blasts (1 sec.)

Standon Vessel Overtaken

1 Short Blast (1 sec.)

2 Short Blasts (1 sec.)

Giveway Vessel Overtaking
...keep clear

1 Short Blast (1 sec.)

International Rules apply outside established lines of demarcation and Inland Rules apply inside the lines. Demarcation lines are printed on most navigational charts and are published in the Navigation Rules.

## Overtaking Situations

2 short blasts (1 sec. each)

2 short blasts (1 sec. each)

**Stand-on Vessel Overtaken**

1 short blast (1 sec. each)

**Give-way Vessel Overtaking ...keep clear**

2 short blasts (1 sec. each)

1 short blast (1 sec. each)

## Crossing Situations

Give-way Vessel
...give way
1 short blast (1 sec.)

Stand-on Vessel
...hold course and speed
1 short blast (1 sec.)

## Meeting Head-On or Nearly So Situations

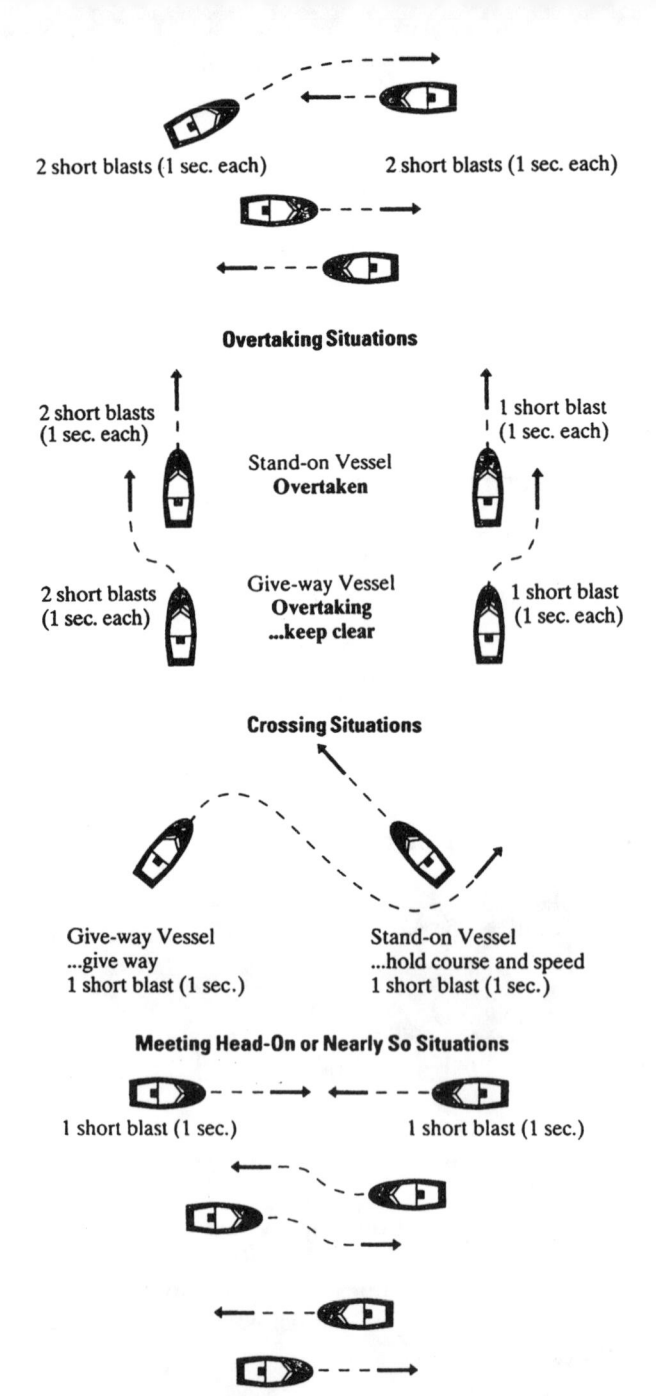

1 short blast (1 sec.)

1 short blast (1 sec.)

Vessels generally pass portside to portside.
However vessels may pass starboard to starboard.

# CHAPTER SEVENTEEN

[SMALL BOAT HANDLING CLASSES ARE VERY INTERESTING, EVEN IF THERE ARE NO BOATS AVAILABLE FOR THE CLASS. HOW DOES THAT GRAB YOU? THEY TELL YOU A WHOLE LOT OF THINGS THAT COULD HAPPEN AND A LOT OF THINGS THAT MIGHT HAPPEN. ALL YOU HAVE TO REMEMBER WHEN IT DOES HAPPEN IS WHAT PAGE IT'S ON AND YOU'LL BE ALL RIGHT. AND IF YOU BELIEVE THAT, I HAVE A GOOD PRICE ON THE BISCAYNE BRIDGE.]

Anyway, Bilge and Betty arrived at the Power Squadron class in high spirits. Some in the class were really high on spirits.

Lo and behold, standing in front of the class with a first class know-it-all look on her face was Ms. Jib Sheets herself, the self-appointed Christ of the sailboats.

"This evening, friends, I'll not call you sailors until after you've heard my lecture on small boat handling. After that you'll get the chance to ask questions and then, you can be positively convinced that I will give you the right answer. In that way, I feel you will have the proper readiness to venture upon the seas. Even if you don't have a sailboat and must ride on a powerboat, you might get the hang of it. You may have noticed I said ride instead of sail on a powerboat. I don't want you to get the idea that I prefer sailboats even if they are the only true way to enjoy the wind and weather, fighting the elements, storms, danger, the . . . "

"Control yourself, for chrissake."

"Who said that? There's a wise ass in this class!"

Ms. Jib Shits [SORRY.] . . . Ms. Jib Sheets stared around the class searching for the powerboat culprit.

All the men in the class took the proper cowardly way out by avoiding her eyes.

"Now we'll have no more of those lowly comments from any friends of that writer. With that said, we can begin. Firstly, we will review passing in a narrow channel.

"Yes, you, the one who looks half-stoned. You ask, what

if you are not in a narrow channel? We will discuss that next but for now try to be on the same channel with the class.

"When vessels are meeting head on or nearly so in a narrow waterway, each vessel is required to give the proper passing signal. One short blast of one second and you direct your course to the starboard and pass port to port; two short blasts and you pass starboard to starboard.

"Yes, you have a problem with that, sir? Pray tell me what is it?"

"Ma'am, I'm the same Half Whats-Going-On as got half of what was going on before. Pray tell me what happens if I hold my finger on the horn button and it comes out two seconds?"

Jib Sheets rolled her eyes and said, "Make three signs of the cross and say 'three Hail Marys' while directing your course to starboard.

"What the hell is that commotion at the back of the class? Yes, you in the back of the class with the curly black hair and being held down by your friend. Oh, you say, he's not your friend. He's your lawyer and he wants you to consult with him before you ask any questions. Well, do it, and let's get on with it."

Struggling to free himself from his lawyer's grip, the brave man made it to his feet. "Lady, what happens if you're Jewish and you hold the button down too long?"

"Well, sir, in your case make three signs of the Star of David, and think dirty thoughts about Yassar Arafat, and of course, direct your course to the starboard. Now what? You think the second part would be easy but the first part would be confusing? Try practicing in front of a mirror.

"Anyway, let's take up one of the most dangerous maneuvers in boating. No sir, I don't mean getting your overweight mother-in-law on the boat. I'm talking about passing in a narrow channel."

"Yes, you, the timid one, who raised one finger instead of your hand. Sorry, you say, you raised two fingers? I'm impressed. Now what the hell do you want? You would rather not ask in front of the whole class? No, sir, you are not going to whisper in my ear, the last guy got off on it.

"Class, please take note that passing signals should never be given unless vessels are in sight of each other. In the fog or in reduced visibility, ships must sound only fog signals.

"You, sir, the third from the right, not you, sir. You are on the left side. Yes, the one with the pain-in-the-ass look on his face. You have something to say? You want to say that's the kind of dumb remark your brother-in-law would make? Mine or yours? Either way I agree with you.

"Now, we will take up the proper way to cross. The vessel having the right of the way used to be called the privileged. It is now known as the stand-on vessel.

"You like what, sir? Please repeat it to the class."

"My name is Ole Codger, and I like the old name even if it don't make any sense, neither."

Jib Sheets replied, "If you don't think that one makes any sense, listen to this. The boat having to keep clear, formerly known as the burdened vessel, is now known as the give-way vessel. Before you ask any questions let me tell you the part of the rules that I think makes the most sense. My beloved sailboats and those useless rowboats normally have the right of way over powerboats. Oooooh! I get off on that.

"Yes, Mrs. Scuppers, you would like to know what the vessel is standing on? It is not standing on anything, Mrs. Scuppers. It's a nautical term. It means that the one with the right of way, or the vessel that is privileged, should keep her course and speed. I must add that no vessel has the right of way through the middle of another.

"You, sir, waving your hand like a child that has to weewee, what's your question?"

"Ma'am, my name is Make-This Shit-Simple. Is we to understand that if'n we don't have the stop sign that we can go like hell up until the time we is going to run over somebody?"

"That is a gross oversimplification, but to the point.

"Yes, Lawyer Quick To-Sue. By the way, sir, you don't have to walk up and down the aisle holding your lapels to ask a question."

"As you say, ma'am. I would like to know under what burden is the burdened vessel suffering under and what civil rights it has to give away?"

"Sir, I think this is not quite the same case that you're trying to make. The give-way vessel only has to give way to the privileged or stand-on vessel so it doesn't get run over."

"Ma'am, my name is Macho Muddle-Headed. What if I got the biggest boat? Shouldn't them suckers get out of my way or get run over?"

"You have a point there, sir, that will put a lot of people in the hospital. But, I notice the gentleman in the back who has been exposed by the class as an insurance spy is jotting down your name. Maybe I can clear this up, class, by explaining the danger zone."

"Yes, Mr. Missed-Something. You want to know how a vessel becomes the privileged vessel? To put it simply, sir, give me a damn chance. Now, the danger zone can be simply explained. Any vessel approaching from dead ahead to two points of abaft the beam on your starboard has the right of way. Simply, if he's on your right and in the ten point arc, that is, from the bow to out your side window, sir, then that vessel has the right of way. Ohhhh, I just love saying this next part. A boat on your left, may be left to pass astern when on your left. Ohhhhhhh!

"Yes, Mr. Scuppers, you don't think you have a bath in your beam? You call it a head on your boat and there's one in the front and one in the back? I don't know why, but I recommend you spend a little more time studying nautical terms, sir.

"Yes, the young lady who is dressed so prim and proper. I just love those horn-rimmed glasses, darling."

"Ma'am, my name is Professor Sails."

"Yes, Professor Sails. I adore that name. Now, class, this is the type of young lady who is capable of asking questions that will further the understanding of the rules of the road and the nautical terms which make our way of life such a wonder to the world. Now, professor, ask your enlightening question."

"Well, Sails is not my real name. It was given to me by my fellow sailors because I'm so quick to spread in the bed. The question which is so paramount in my mind is, is there any more toilet paper for the head?"

"Sit down, idiot! Now, let's review a situation that is often frightening to new mariners but must be addressed. It's called overtaking and passing a vessel in a narrow channel. When overtaking a vessel that is slower than your vessel and you wish to pass, the vessel in front of you is the stand-on vessel and you are the give-way vessel. If you wish to pass him on his starboard side which is your port side, you sound one blast of the whistle and pass your port to his starboard. Of course, that's just the opposite if you want to pass on the other side.

"No sir, Mr. Macho Muddle-Head. If he doesn't answer your signal, you don't get on the radio and tell him to get the hell out of the way or you'll kick his ass. Another thing, class, this habit of shooting the bird to slower sailboats who refuse to move out of the way but do eventually let you go by, I think, is a disgusting mannerism. Remember, we may be slower but we are in front and most of us sail-boaty types are not only the privileged vessel but the privileged people. And we think this privil. . ."

From the back of the class, "Give us a damn break, will you?"

Ms. Jib Sheets eye-balled the class and remarked, "I think there's a wise ass powerboat operator somewhere here in this class. Anyway, Mr. Make This Shit-Simple, you suggest blowing your horn repeatedly? Then, when the other guy moves over for you to go around? That's close, but not entirely accurate.

"Mrs. Scuppers, you have something to say? You made up a little poem? Good, let's hear it."

Betty stood up and curtsied to the class. "One tootie toot to the right, and you're right to go right. Two tootie toots to the left, and you're left to go left. Your one tootie toot makes him go left and your two tootie toots makes him go right. You follow your tootie toot, he follows his tootie toot and everybody goes tootie toot, merrily, merrily gently down the stream."

After a round of applause and many bravos, Betty curtsied once again, blushed and sat down. Ms. Jib Sheets walked over, knelt in the corner and thanked God she got it across.

"Class, we have a surprise for you. One of the problems

confronting mariners is the proper use of the radio. We have a special guest tonight to explain the proper use of the VHF MF equipment.

"No sir, you with the stupid grin on your face, that's not the M. F. VHF. It's the other way around.

"Lawyer Quick To-Sue, you have a pertinent question to ask before we proceed with the radio? Go right ahead, sir. Thank you for not walking down the aisle, but you may hold your lapels. You say you would like to know in these passing situations if there is such a thing as whiplash in boating? Well, one of my sailing partners is into black leather jackets, handcuffs, and silk whips. And you do occasionally get a few lash marks. You weren't referring to that kind of whiplash? You mean the type you get when you are rear-ended in a car. You're into some kinky stuff, sir. You say I sound like a floating sex maniac? Sir, it's you with all the dirty questions.

"Anyway, let me introduce Mr. Stutterbound, our guest instructor for the evening lecturing on the use of the radio."

"My my my name name name is is as she said Sssttuutterbbbound. I I bbrougght my mmike alllong sooo I wouldn't stutter. When I got this thhhhhing in my hand, I speak almost normal."

Mr. Stutterbound placed the mike in front of his mouth even though it wasn't attached to anything, pressed the button, and was born again.

"The proper use of channel sixteen is, remember, it ain't no damn socializing channel. But, you'll notice by far, it's the one most socialized on. Think of it this way, pilgrims. Channel sixteen is the hot line for search and rescue. Avoid excessive calls."

"Sir, my name is Miss Terrified Of-Boats. If you need to be searched and rescued, why must you avoid excessive calling? My question is, am I limited to screaming once for help or twice?"

"Tain't a damn thing of what I mean, lady. You're supposed to avoid excess.

"Mr. Quick To-Sue, you say there are various interpretations of the word, excess? To elaborate on your previous statement, sir, I don't give a rat's ass.

"All right now, let's clarify this excessive calling. You may call three times at two minute intervals then wait fifteen minutes before calling again. I interpret it this way, if your boat hasn't sunk within that fifteen-minute interval, you get to scream for help again. Now, here's the one I been working on for a long time and ain't figured out how to do it yet. It says right here in this book. I said that so you won't think I thought up such a thing, 'To schedule your calls to other vessels in advance'. Wait! Hell, there's more. 'This will help you avoid calling persons who are not listening'. Ain't that the pits!"

"Sir, my name is What If-I-Goof. What if you don't know the hutter fellow on the hutter vessel you is a'calling? Won't that cause a little problem in the scheduling?"

"Man, don't ask me. I don't know nothin'. I'm just teaching this class. Anyhow, does anybody know how to figure this one out?"

Betty rose and said, "Mr. Teacher Man, I think I know the answer."

"Get on it, baby. I need to know."

"Weellllll, from a lady's point of view, the first part goes like this. When you are going to call someone you know, call them and tell them when you are going to call them. Annnnnd, the second part is about talking to someone who is not listening. That's easy, just try talking to your husband when he is watching football. You are talking to somebody but he is definitely not listening."

"Hell, I should have asked my wife a long time ago, but she is more into yelling at me than talking when I'm watching football."

Lots of "She is sooo right," from the ladies, and "What the hell is she talking about?" from the men.

"There is one more subject I'm going to subject you to and that is, repeating-back information given by the sending vessel that is unnecessary and much more, it's superfluous. Ain't that word something?"

"I'm Mr. What If-I-Goof again, and what if the Coast Guard don't get to the proper spot where you're sinking on your first screaming? Don't it make sense to just keep on screaming?"

Stutterbound bristled with anger saying, "Listen here, fool. If you keep up all that panicking when you are about to drown how is the Coast Guard going to find your body, anyway? Their job is hard enough without you making it more difficult.

"I'm gonna put this mike down 'now. . . . . . . . . . . . . . . .
. . . th . . . th . . . th . . . that's all, fo . . . fo . . . fo . . . folks."

Jib Sheets returned to the front of the class, surveyed the group with her evil eye and said, "Now we are going to go over some of the nautical terms and dress which are so necessary to good boating. We, the true sailors on sailboats, all know the proper terms, so I am speaking to the retarded, I mean, in nautical terms, the powerboat people.

"First, let's start at your bottoms."

Betty whispered, "Bilge, you already know about bottom wear."

Jib Sheets, with her all-encompassing eye surveyed the class and said, "They're called footwear, not shoes. Ladies should never wear high heels on a boat." Betty hid her feet under the seat.

"Both men and women should wear rubber soles without heels." Bilge hid his patent leather shoes under his seat.

"Now for clothing. Gentlemen, it's all right to wear your blazers on special occasions but not all the time." Bilge wished he could hide all together.

"Wear loose clothes, wind-breakers, dungarees that are salt-worn and holed . . . southwesters to stand against the rough seas, grabbing onto the riggings to fight the waves, standing against the . . ."

"Turn that crap off, for chrissakes!"

Jib Sheets screamed, "That damn porno-thinking Know-It-All writer is here someplace. I just know it. Now that we are properly clothed, let's turn to the subject of guests aboard. Again, firstly, show your guests aboard, then show them about the boat. That is, both below and above. Take these moments to explain the full terminology of boating such as, 'that's port and the other side is starboard'. This will not be necessary for sailboat people . . . WE already know.

"Explain completely the use of a head on the boat. You

might try, 'doodoo and wee wee, and push this button' and 'if you throw anything in the head that won't flush, you get to dive over and get it out.' Simply put, sailors, if it doesn't come out of your body, it doesn't go down the head. Except for the toilet paper you asked about, Professor Sails."

"Miss Jib Sheets, I'm What If-I-Goof, again. What if you have to pee on one of them sailboats and they is leaning over in the wind like I seen them? And what if you have to do the other thing?"

"Well, a good sailor learns to hold on to things besides the riggings all day, if you know what I mean."

"What if I don't know what you mean?"

"When you're down below tinkling, try a bank shot off the side of the potty. If you have the other urge, tie your ass to the seat and have at it."

Ms. Jib Sheets requested, "Lady, where are you going and why are you pulling your husband by the ear? You say, you're going to hurry and try to get your deposit back on the sailboat your husband is going to buy? Coward. I do not appreciate your parting finger gesture, lady. Now that the What-Ifs are gone, it pays to give each guest a job. Don't make it anything worthwhile. Something like 'stand by this bit in case it jumps overboard.' This keeps your guests out of the way.

"Nextly, show the men where the binoculars are so they won't fall overboard or get eyestrain from trying to see the girls' boobs on the other boats. Make sure you give these grownups time limits so they won't choke each other over their turn.

"Anotherly... don't let your guests dive overboard unless the boat is at anchor or they might drown before you get back. Another point on this which has two points: make sure your boat is in the water before they dive overboard or is in enough water to keep them from sticking their heads in the sand.

"Importantly, keep a supply of foul-weather gear aboard for all guests. The pleasure of sailing into a rainstorm can be marred by wet freezing guests going down below to puke all over your bunks. Keep them dry. Expose them to the wind, rain, seas, lightening, the . . ."

"Stop the crap, will ya, Jib Shits?"

"He's here. I can feel it in my bones. That Know-It-All, powerboat sucker is here someplace."

"Anyway, seasickness is not a contagious disease, even if one guest sees the other puke and they all start. Pack all the suspects with Dramamine and go. Oh, make sure you explain windward and leeward. Peeing and puking from the wrong side of the boat tends to make a guest unwelcomed on the return trip to port. Remember, sailors, one hand for yourself and one hand for the boat. No, you sicko, it's not what you are thinking.

"The first rule in boating is that a skipper must be the skipper at all times. A good study of this is my choice 'Mutiny On The Bounty' and 'Lady Chatterley's Lover'.

"Some safety tips about guests. If children are aboard, keep them in strait jackets, sorry, life jackets.

"Once morely, if anybody falls overboard the skipper should not be the one to jump overboard to save him. The damn boat will be a mile away before someone figures out what to do. The proper thing to do for the victim is throw him something or somebody that will float. Then, return and try to get him out of the water without running over whoever or whatever is still floating.

"Class, our secondly mostest important guest is Mr. Quick-To-Cancel, your friendly boat insurance man, I think. Class, don't let his mascara and false eyelashes lead you astray. He knows insurance from his top to his bottom."

Mr. Quick-To-Cancel sashayed to the podium and said, "Oooohhh, I love it. Listen, darlings. Make sure when you anchor that you don't do it in a ship channel. Not too long ago some fools anchored in the channel at Lake Worth and caused a mess with our fair trading partner, the Japanese." Bilge and Betty were looking for a place to hide if their names were mentioned.

"And you macho honeys, don't throw your anchor overboard. Someone may be standing in the coils of the line. And splash! Over they go with the anchor. Oh, yes, put a light on your boat at night. Remember, no light on the boat, no boat in the morning. It also goes to show you, no boat, no you.

"When you sailors anchor your boats at night, which I

notice is damn near on top of each other, make sure you put out enough line. This should be done regardless of how much room there is in the anchorage. If you have to fend off your neighbor who doesn't want to go through the trouble of using enough anchor line and he starts to drag, don't use your boat hook as a lance to fend him off. One fellow used his hook for a lance to fend off another boat. He placed it against his belly with his back against the deck house; consequently he was skewered. My advice is to use your bumpers and curse the hell out of the other guy.

"Well, that's all I have for you, darlings. Except you, no, the timid one with the two fingers raised. See me after class, will you?"

Ms. Jib Sheets returned to the podium and was all smiles. She said, "Class, this is the last session in boating instruction and we want to honor two people who have endured the whole suffering mess. Sorry about that. That damn crazy Know-It-All writer put those words in my mouth. I would never have said out loud what I was thinking. What I meant to say was, to honor two people who have endured the whole pleasant experience. We have a little plaque with their names on it saying, 'To two who endured'. Will Bilge and Betty Scuppers come forward to receive their plaque?"

Bilge stood and bowed to Betty. She curtsied and they walked proudly on Cloud Sixteen to the front of the class. On receiving their plaque, Bilge made a speech. "I know boating is much safer now that this class is going to be out there, cruising the waters, fighting the elements, dodging each other, trying to get bridges to open, sailing out on stormy seas . . ."

Betty exclaimed, "Holy diggity dog, pooty poo! Bilge has got the boat bug. Shut up already, Bilge. I'm catching it too!"

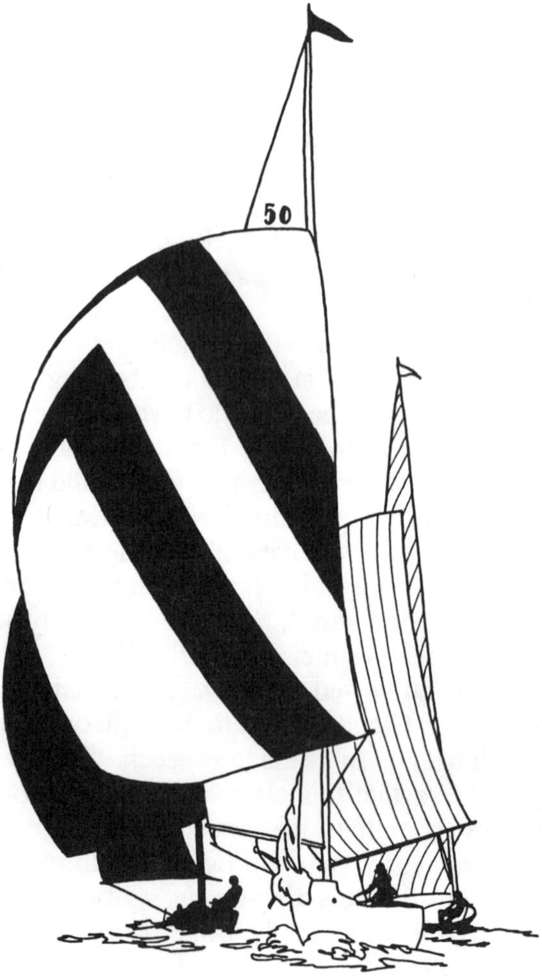
50

# CHAPTER EIGHTEEN

Anyway Bilge "boat bug" and Betty "I've got the boat bug, too" returned to MY MISTAKE full of pride. Late evening lights beckoned on the bay, soft music serenaded them, drinky poos were served, and Bilge was full of enthusiasm.

"Betty, we did it, me and you babe, all by ourselves. Can you believe, we got the plaque!"

"Oh Bilge, we are sailors at last, I'm so proud of us. You knowing half of what is going on and me knowing the other half of what is going on, we sure will make one big whole on the water and we have the plaque to prove it."

"Betty, know what I'm thinking?"

"Are you thinking what I'm thinking that you are thinking what I'm thinking about, captain?"

"That's what I'm thinking, first and only mate. Gee, it's nice when you know what I'm thinking."

Bilge stood stiffly. Walked to the bow pulpit. Raised his glass to the world. Placed his hand inside his blazer in a Napoleonic stance and exclaimed, "To the Keys!"

Caught up in the moment, Betty squealed, "To the Keys!"

As Bilge placed his arm around Betty, he declared, "Sailing off into danger, dodging whales, fighting storms, finding treasure, and best of all we're real people now. First class sailors, not some silly characters in a crazy book. You know Betty, we can go anywhere in the world without that damn Know-It-All writer telling stories about us."

Betty squealed again, "Yeah, no damn Know-It-All writer telling stories about us. We're real people now!"

"Betty, do you want to go below and practice some of that other kind of mating?"

"Oooooohhhhh, Bilge. You're soooooo romantic."

---

[A NOTE FROM THE KNOW-IT-ALL WRITER: "I'LL

GET YOU TWO FOR THAT! YOU'RE NOT GOING ANY PLACE WITHOUT ME. SO THERE!]

THIS IS NOT THE END...BUT THE BEGINNING!

*Get ready to duck! Another adventure of Bilge & Betty is on its way! Carlo D. Hapol.*

**COMING SOON:**

BILGE AND BETTY SCUPPERS TO THE KEYS!

**A REQUEST FROM THE AUTHOR:**

If you would like to share any of your sea stories for the next sequel featuring Bilge and Betty Scuppers, please address them to the publisher.

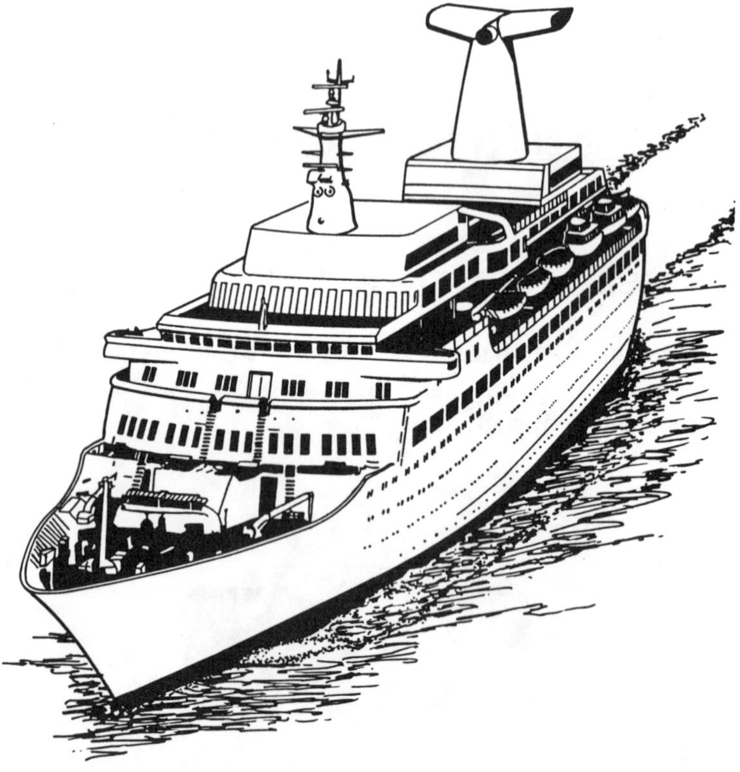

# ORDER FORM

| | |
|---|---|
| **How They Owned a Boat and Didn't Spend Any Money** | $9.95 |
| **Cooking Country with Shotgun Red** | $15.95 |
| **The Cajun Gourmet Afloat and On the Road** | $15.95 |
| **All I Ever Wanted to Know About Cooking I Learned From Momma** | $14.95 |
| **The Upper Crud Cookbook** | $15.95 |
| **Is This Country Cooking? This is Country Cooking!** | $15.95 |
| **The Wing'ed Whale from Woefully** | $14.95 |

Please select your choice of books and add $2.75 per book for shipping and packaging. *Send to:*

**HAWK PUBLISHING AND DISTRIBUTING**
P.O. Box 8422
Longboat Key, FL 34228

*Mail Books To:*

Name _____

Address _____

City _____ State _____ Zip _____